An OPUS book

# MODERN THEOLOGY

## A Sense of Direction

OPUS General Editors

Keith Thomas
Alan Ryan
Walter Bodmer

OPUS books provide concise, original, and authoritative introductions to a wide range of subjects in the humanities and sciences. They are written by experts for the general reader as well as for students.

# Modern Theology

## A Sense of Direction

JAMES P. MACKEY

Oxford   New York

OXFORD UNIVERSITY PRESS

1987

Oxford University Press, Walton Street, Oxford OX2 6DP

Oxford  New York  Toronto
Delhi  Bombay  Calcutta  Madras  Karachi
Petaling Jaya  Singapore  Hong Kong  Tokyo
Nairobi  Dar es Salaam  Cape Town
Melbourne  Auckland

and associated companies in
Beirut  Berlin  Ibadan  Nicosia

Oxford is a trade mark of Oxford University Press

British Library Cataloguing in Publication Data
Mackey, James P.
Modern theology: a sense of direction.—(OPUS)
1. Theology, Doctrinal
I. Title  II. Series
230  BT77.3
ISBN 0–19–219220–5
ISBN 0–19–289206–1 Pbk

Library of Congress Cataloging in Publication Data
Mackey, James Patrick.
Modern theology. (OPUS)
Bibliography: p.
1. Theology——20th century.  2. Christianity——Philosophy.
3. Jesus Christ——Person and offices.
I. Title.  II. Series.
BT28.M237 1987   230'.09'04   86–23770
ISBN 0–19–219220–5
ISBN 0–19–289206–1 (pbk.)

Set by Colset Private Limited
Printed in Great Britain by
The Guernsey Press Co. Ltd.
Guernsey, Channel Islands

# Contents

# 1
# Jesus and the Christian Religion

One of the key problems facing Christianity today is the problem of the relationship of the religion to its alleged founder. I have to write 'alleged founder' because this is precisely the problem: did Jesus of Nazareth in any acceptable sense of the word found the religion which more than a millennium and a half after his death Europe knew as Christianity, and which in the successive centuries of the next half millennium European traders, missionaries and *conquistadores* spread vigorously over the rest of the earth? Did he even found the religion which the Protestant Reformers of the sixteenth century claimed was more in conformity with his teaching, and which their missionaries then spread abroad using much the same methods? This is a key problem in its own right, and also in the sense that it opens up so many other issues of importance to modern theology, about God and incarnation, about faith and revelation.

Some modern writers have raised the problem explicitly. It has been suggested, for example, that Paul of Tarsus, rather than Jesus, was the real founder of Christianity because it was he, and not Jesus, who introduced the figure of a pre-existent divine being, and he who identified this being with Jesus. Other writers have raised the question of whether, in Herbert Butterfield's words, Jesus himself was perhaps no more than a myth, or possibly even a syndicate. These more radical proposals have, however, made a less lasting impact on modern thought than those movements which have raised more implicitly the problem of Jesus's relationship to the Christian religion.

There are basically three such movements, though they are closely interconnected: the quest for the historical Jesus; the more general discussion of the relationship between history, with its perennially provisional results, and faith, with its constant anxiety for absolute assurance; and the progress of recent

European philosophy which, with the exception of some insular examples such as British empiricism, moves in the lengthening shadow of Hegel, and is characterized by the rediscovery of the temporality of being. The first of these is the easiest to describe which is the sole reason why it is listed first; the remaining two are increasingly difficult.

Indeed, the third movement, linked as it is with the philosophies of men such as Heidegger and Gadamer, is so difficult to describe that it might well seem an unreasonable hurdle in the opening chapter of a book written for a series which aims to provide stimulating and authoritative introductions to chosen subjects.

Heidegger, however, for a self-professed non-believer, had an enormous influence upon modern theology, on Protestant theology mainly through Bultmann, and on Catholic theology principally through Rahner. In addition, the first chapter seeks ways of talking about religious faith and of identifying a particular form of it, while the second chapter considers the possibility that religious faith, like other forms of knowledge or 'rational belief', may be as much a matter of practice as of 'pure' theory. And the pervasive influence of Hegel comes as surely through Heidegger and Gadamer to modern attempts to deal with the subject-matter of the first chapter, as it comes through Feuerbach and Marx to modern analysis of the topic of the second chapter.

Great and influential philosophers give definitive expression to the spiritual mood of the age in which they live, if they do not in fact create that mood. It would be possible to write an introduction to modern theology while omitting Heidegger, and the section on the temporality of being. But then we should never see the true depth and significance of the first two movements. For, whatever else one may say about those who have sought the historical Jesus, they were searching for God in this world and its history as human reason understands these; they were searching for God in time and memory. And we need to know whether they were defeated by those who tried to keep divine revelation and human faith safe from the vicissitudes of history, or whether time-consumed existence, always apparently hastening towards annihilation, still holds out hope for them. Heidegger is the philosopher *par excellence* of *Being and Time*. One could introduce modern theology without mentioning him, but the introduction could never claim to be in the least authoritative.

## The Quest for the Historical Jesus

The modern quest for the historical Jesus is now some 200 years old. Its stated aim was to replace the dogmatic portrait of Jesus— in particular doctrines about his divine status—with a truly and 'scientifically' historical portrait of the actual man who was born in obscure circumstances somewhere in Galilee and executed by Pontius Pilate as a messianic pretender in Jerusalem around the year 27 on our present Christian calendar. The early results of the quest proved to be a profusion of portraits, differing from each other in quite substantial detail. (The reader who wishes to be convinced of this historical fact need only turn to a masterpiece which the sheer passage of time has made into an interim report, Albert Schweitzer's *The Quest of the Historical Jesus*.) Yet even when, in the early decades of the present century, the quest itself was frequently discredited, the number of portraits of Jesus still continued to multiply. An instructive example is to be found in the study of the titles of Jesus in the New Testament.

### *Jesus' New Testament titles*

A great many titles are conferred upon Jesus in the New Testament: Christ (Messiah, Annointed One), which later come to be used like part of his proper name (Jesus Christ), Lord, Son of God, Son of Man, Word, Rabbi, Saviour, Prophet. Though most of the many books devoted to these titles agree that they tell us first and foremost what his followers thought of Jesus, almost all of them were additionally intent on discovering which title or titles most accurately described who or what he actually was; some went further still and tried to say which, if any, of these titles Jesus himself used in self-designation. But this project, like others which were also less ambitious in scope than the grand quest—the search for the authentic sayings of Jesus, for example, or for his actual deeds—served initially only to increase the confusion of portraits, if only because of the level of disagreement which now appears to be endemic to New Testament scholarship.

The promise which the titles appeared to hold out for the success of the quest derived from the view that each title denotes a specific role. This promise, however, was dimmed by the dawning realization that the titles themselves, all of them borrowed, were already susceptible to quite a variety of interpretations, and that all had had to be further reshaped in order to cover the unexpected and unwelcome figure of Jesus. Just how much any of them needed to be reshaped was and still is quite difficult to determine, however, because the very attraction of titles is their ability to categorize the recipient within some familiar role, and the suspicion must always be present, therefore, that those who confer titles wish to have the recipient on their terms rather than his.

The opening of one of the earliest authoritative texts of the Christian tradition, attributed to a man named Mark, 'The beginning of the gospel of Jesus Christ, the Son of God', can be reliably interpreted to mean that the story which follows is the glad proclamation, the presentation, of the Son of God; that is to say that the universally misunderstood and rejected man who now appears on stage and disappears from it on being killed (for Mark has no subsequent 'appearance' stories) is already the only Son of God we may know. Here, in the earliest Christian literature, we find already a passionate polemic against those who wanted a more heavenly Son of God, safe from the vicissitudes of history.

Long after New Testament times, titles continue to exercise their attraction. Men as far apart in climate and culture as Patrick Pearse in my own country and Camilo Torres in Colombia have depicted Jesus Christ as Liberator in a role that conforms remarkably to their own self-sacrificing revolutionary zeal. In more scholarly ranks Jesus the Hasid, the miracle-working holy man, might be preferred, since Jewish scholarship in particular can now document such a historical role and date it to the time of Jesus. From the Byzantine Emperor of the Cosmos to Jesus Christ Superstar, such titles have allowed people of vastly different backgrounds and widely differing hopes and expectations to identify Jesus, and at times even to identify with him. But the complaint which Albert Schweitzer made against the questers applies also to all lesser projects: that the resulting portraits seem to be just as dogmatic as the dogmatic portrait which modern historical technique was supposed to replace.

None of this, of course, makes it any easier to find a solution to the original problem of the relationship of the Christian religion to its alleged founder. On the contrary, it almost seems as if any number of religions or quasi-religions could be founded with little more in common than an appeal to the name Jesus Christ. Perhaps that is too harsh; perhaps in all this historical and possible variety there is always some Wittgensteinian set of family resemblances. What is clear, however, is that the confusion of portraits which results from historical quests both great and small, far from solving our original problem, is related most intimately to a more general problem, the topic of the second modern movement mentioned: the relationship between faith and history.

## Faith and History

Faith, wrote Rudolf Bultmann in what must surely be one of his best-remembered pronouncements, cannot be made to depend upon the historian's labours. That certainly has the strong, clean lines of a pronouncement intended to be definitive, but what precisely is it meant to convey? When dealing with a genius as original and as complex as Bultmann, one must not look for too simple an answer. He is almost as much indebted to the spirit of contemporary philosophical thought in his expressions of Christian belief as he is to the central conviction of his Reformed tradition that salvation is by faith alone, and does not need the support of works, not even the works of reason, not even in the guise of the modern historian. Certainly he is not a simple sceptic about the prospects of the modern science of history in attempting to distil some reliable facts about Jesus from extant Christian sources; on the contrary, he is as willing as the next scholar to rest his reputation upon his own selection of alleged facts. But he is still adamant that Christian faith must not be made to depend upon them, nor can his adamance be attributed solely to his allegiance to the Reformers' principle of salvation by faith alone.

It seems rather that his view of history is modelled on that dominant image of empirical science which has so utterly dominated theories of knowledge since it first began to record its quite remarkable successes some four centuries ago. Created in this image, history too must accumulate objective data, propose its hypotheses, and test these against both available data and data yet to be acquired. Faith, however, cannot be forever provisional. It is not, as Kierkegaard would say, a matter of approximation. It cannot, therefore, be made to depend upon a historian's labours.

Herbert Butterfield approached the relationship of *Christianity and History* (the title of one of his books) from the point of view of the professional historian. He, too, is insistent that technical history, with its proper apparatus and its evidences, can offer neither moral values nor religious vision. Its results must be available, indeed equally accessible, to all, whether atheist or theist, Muslim, Hindu, or Christian. The prophet, the theologian, and the philosopher (the poet too, he adds, and that will be of interest to us shortly) must bring their interpretations to history and superimpose these upon it.

History can do a number of things for Christian faith. First, it can challenge and correct what Butterfield calls ecclesiastical interpretations of history, which are but examples of those distortions of the past which mask the interests of all kinds of social institutions, too often to the detriment of the genuine interests of human kind.

Second, from the more extensive surveys of successive civilizations we can learn some general lessons about the human condition such that it can be seen that the Christian interpretation 'fits' rather well. As Butterfield himself says, he is convinced from his broad studies that the general course of history is so shaped that a Christian is in the right relation to it.

Third, since he is not so committed to unqualified openness and provisionality as Bultmann appears to be, and since he is convinced that some historical facts are now sufficiently attested to make them safe for all future assertion, he is prepared to concede what Bultmann too should surely have conceded, namely, that some facts must be historically secure if Christianity's claims are not altogether to fail. The existence of Jesus for Butterfield, and his crucifixion for Bultmann, are minimal examples of such facts.

Finally, from the perspective of philosophical theology, Van Harvey's book, *The Historian and the Believer*, offers the most detailed analysis of both the believer's convictions and the historian's conclusions. Harvey, too, joins the chorus and chants the familiar lines about the clear difference between faith's penchant for absolute conviction and history's forever provisional, always probable—even if at times very highly probable—results. He accepts the need for Christians to try to ascertain some historical facts about the founder of their faith, and at the end of the book he suggests a sequence of subjects of inquiry and some final thoughts on how they are to be related: (1), the actual Jesus who lies behind (2), the historical Jesus, who is the Jesus now recoverable by historical means, but recoverable it would seem only through (3), the perspectival image or memory impression of Jesus which is contained almost exclusively in the New Testament, and (4), the biblical Christ.

The memory impression is already the result of a highly selective interpretation of Jesus as a significant 'event' in the lives of those who met him; yet even if we adhere to the 'morality' of historical research and acknowledge the tentative nature of its results, this can still yield some very high probabilities about the historical Jesus. The biblical Christ, on the other hand, represents a *transformation* in our image of Jesus whereby he becomes the medium of divine revelation and salvation. While it may well be possible to find some correlation between the memory impression of the historical Jesus and the biblical Christ—in that the historical Jesus, let us say, tried to bring people to religious decision and the biblical Christ, accepted or rejected, implies a quite similar religious decision—faith is not, according to Harvey, dependent upon such a correlation, however much the modern mind may prefer to look to historical figures for the symbols of its faith. Religious faith relates us to present reality and finds its particular certitude in the success with which it does so. Historical probabilities do not contribute to such certitude, however much they may help in other ways to illustrate its content.

The overall impression gained from this modern discussion of the relationship between history and faith is that history, in its modern scientific mode, can establish some facts about Jesus of Nazareth with reasonable certainty, but that faith cannot be derived from them. Faith, with its own complement of quite specific convictions, can be offered as an interpretation of these historical facts; it can be laid alongside them so that correlations of claim or image can be noted or, as Butterfield puts it, it can be superimposed on them. But—the point is repeated from author to author—faith cannot be derived from them. If this is the true relationship between history and faith, it is small wonder that the quest for the historical Jesus could not help us to decide if Jesus truly founded the faith that still to this day claims him for itself.

## Why we must challenge the dichotomy between history and faith

So why not let the matter rest? Why not be satisfied with the minimum of historical fact which does seem secure for future assertion? Why not be content with what Bultmann, with the literary inelegance so typical of German theology, called the 'that' of Jesus?

After all, other religions which look to historical founders treat these founders simply as channels of divine revelation. The revelation is the thing; faith the proper response to it. The revelation contains all the knowledge of God and of his will that is necessary for the highest human hopes; faith appropriates it now as completely as when it first arrived. The 'that' of Muhammad, of Guru Nanak, of Baha'ullah, is by comparison a matter of mere historical fact. For Christians, too, to claim Jesus for their faith is merely a way of asserting that the true, definitive revelation from God is the one which in fact came through Jesus. It is merely a matter of identifying by means of the channel through which it came the final revelation of God's will, which Christian faith must now appropriate—and there follows an account of the content of this revelation, a particular knowledge of God and of the divine will. So why not simply accept the dichotomy of faith and history?

The simple answer is that too much is already at stake—so much so that a difficult wrestling with notions of history and faith may be the only faithful response to the intellectual challenge with which the quest for the historical Jesus still faces us. It is even difficult to indicate at this stage all that may be at stake, but some attempt to do so may at least help to illustrate how our opening problem provides in fact a key to many others.

What do Christians mean by incarnation? An unchanging, invulnerable, divine 'substance' (as Augustine would say), joined in some mysterious but 'personal' way to a very vulnerable human frame, and using the latter to transmit the Message, and perhaps also to perform some astounding deeds to prove its presence? Or did divinity actually *become* fully human, as we all of us understand the human condition? And if the latter, why *cannot* history lay hold on incarnation? Can history, or can it not, lay hold on the human?

What do Christians think of God? Infinitely other, as the jargon sometimes has it, sending out irresistible Word to fashion, instruct, judge? Or something like a more immanent and all-pervasive grace, keeping faith with those who have broken faith with her, and unwilling to evade even the experience of death?

Divinity is always held to be transcendent. But divinity must also be immanent, however indirectly or fleetingly so, and it is the kind and quality of immanence claimed in a particular faith which determines, surely, whether history can lay hold on alleged traces of the divine, or only on the unsupportable assertions of self-proclaimed believers.

Does Christianity have a revelation, delivered and sealed once for all by God? Or was the human being in whom God became human a man who like all of us lived by faith and, unlike most of us, died keeping faith with unconditioned grace? The answer to this question looks forward to the next chapter where faith is said to be a 'way' that one walks and the rites of passage are described; it looks back to the earlier questions of how Christians understand incarnation and think of God; and it raises some very insistent doubts, for Christians at any rate, about the wisdom of settling so easily for a simple sharing-out of assertions between something called history and something called faith.

There seems no option, then, but to challenge the dichotomous distinction between history and faith. Fortunately, the third modern movement provides us with the means to challenge it. But we may as well be warned in advance that help from this quarter carries a heavy price, for the leaders of this movement all eschew religious faith as such. With their help we might find the historical Jesus alright, but only as the founder of a very human faith which proves in the end to be an illusion. However, one step at a time. First, overcome this dichotomy between history and faith, and then see if there really is no prospect of a *religious* faith that is born, lives, and grows within the very texture of historical existence.

It seems probable that the crippling dichotomy between history and faith owes much of its continued survival to a naïve view of the nature of empirical science, which has been the product of philosophers rather than scientists and which still wields a certain influence despite more recent attempts in the philosophy of science to get rid of it. According to this naïve view there are facts lying about in the past for the historian to discover, just as there are particles lying about all over the place for physicists to discover. In both cases these are data, simply given. They can be perceived according to a naïve-realist view of perception; their accumulation will suggest hypothetical categories, relationships, theories, which can both direct the scientist where to look further and serve to confirm or correct the original hypothesis. The categories, relationships, and theories are all generated, and improved, corrected, or cancelled, by the accumulation of data objectively perceived without interpretation.

According to this view an empirical process may never yield more than probability, but it yields all the truth of which we humans are capable. This is the kind of position presented in A. J. Ayer's *Language Truth and Logic*, a book which brought the British empiricist tradition to a hitherto unsuspected degree of sheer naïvety. It is the kind of position which prompted Anthony Flew to affirm that the exponentially growing achievements of modern science have done more than anything else to spread the naturalistic world outlook which is the almost inevitable setting for some form of atheism. It therefore lends considerable credence to the view that the dichotomy between history and faith with which we have been dealing is in fact the fag-end of a kind of rationalism which took this false philosophical model of modern science as the paradigm of all true knowledge, and relegated all other convictions to the realm of mere beliefs—though it was allowed that some of these beliefs were urged upon us by the very best of our moral endeavours and might in turn be thought to support these endeavours. The dichotomy between history and faith does not, of course, entail any such relegation of religious faith in the case of the writers we have been looking at, but it does still leave us with a questionable view of history, and with two very different kinds of knowing which we then have the greatest difficulty in relating to each other, to the detriment of both.

## Being and Time

So let us plunge into the third and most difficult of our modern movements and go straight to Heidegger, the single most influential philosopher, after Hegel, in this century—certainly as far as theology is concerned, for it was Heidegger who maintained most stoutly that historical knowledge transcends the idea of rigour held in the exact sciences, and in fact comes closest to that primordial kind of knowing which actually constitutes the very character of our human existence in the world.

### Heidegger's There-being

Possibly the best way to read Heidegger is to pretend that one is reading science fiction. Not that there is anything fictional about his analysis of human existence; but it helps to get one used to the odd jargon and prepares one for the strangeness of an existence that we so unthinkingly take to be so familiar. So, instead of meeting the Everyman of the medieval mystery plays one meets a character called There-being (in German, *Dasein*, a much more friendly sounding name). There-being is Everyman, and he comes to disclose every man's inescapable predicament and every man's hope. Questioned about himself he will first describe himself as thrown-project, which means firstly that he found himself dumped in this world. Now if that were all that his self-description meant he might have been called thrown-there, but in fact it means much more. For he does not find himself dumped in a world which is totally unfamiliar to him; on the contrary, he appears, mysteriously perhaps, to have a kind of prepossession of it (*Vorhabe*, in his own language), a preconception (*Vorgriff*), almost a kind of foresight (*Vorsicht*). Nor is he just dumped there as an inert extra. He is a *project* in this world, which he somehow already knows.

It is only in this kind of analysis that There-being can keep these two aspects of himself apart. In his actual experience, his preconceptions of the world and his conscious projects in and for it are as continuous and inseparable as artificially designated segments of the unbroken line of a circle. Indeed, if one were to think of his circle as a living, moving circle, one could say perhaps that they flow into each other perpetually. Heidegger called this primordial way of knowing 'understanding', and it is There-being's characteristic mode of existence. It defines the kind of entity which There-being happens to be. It must be assimilated by those who want to understand him before any other distinctions are introduced, between subject and object, for instance, or between theory and practice, or between science, art, and morality, for all these are subsequent distinctions.

The description thrown-project—again it sounds more ono-matopoeic in his own language as *geworfene Entwurf*—does not, however, say everything about There-being. In fact it does not even fully explain his name, or reveal all the cleverness, the verbal adroitness, hidden in that choice of name. For There-being is adamant that in describing the circle of understanding which defines his unique mode of existence, he is not just looking into consciousness or mind, into a subject as distinct from an object, such that he might be thought to be describing subjective states and imposing these upon some alien reality. On the contrary, he insists that in the circle of understanding which thrown-project describes, and which is his unique mode of existence, something called 'being' is coming to reflective consciousness, coming to expression. The structure revealed by the phrase thrown-project, in particular the structure of temporality, the moving, living drama of prepossessing in the process of projecting (the future), of projecting the prepossessed (past), is thus the structure, the drama, of being itself. (Hence, Heidegger's masterpiece is called *Being and Time*.) So There-being is there for being and being is there in There-being, since it is there that being comes to expression. A very suggestive name, one must admit.

Now, of course, one needs to question There-being further on the use of this word 'being'. Used with such comprehensive meaning, with such a limitless range of reference, being is not a word in common usage—though it is a word which comes naturally enough on a little exposure to philosophical reflection. But it might first be useful to reflect further on some elements of There-being's explanation so far.

First, let us look at this preconception which There-being claims, if only in the process of projecting, of establishing a conscious project in the world. Partly for future reference and partly because such dualisms as knowing and acting, theory and practice, mind and body, subjective and objective, may press their unwelcome distortions upon us even at this early stage, something should now be said about the *bodily* nature of this preconception-in-project.

It was Maurice Merleau-Ponty who proposed in his *Phenomenology of Perception* the fundamental role of *bodily* presence and projection in our primordial knowledge of the world. I thought at first that it might be difficult to produce an example of bodily knowing which would not simply repeat one of his, and then it suddenly dawned on me that I quite literally had one at my fingertips. For as I sit at my microcomputer my fingers know how to communicate these words to you. And it is in a very real sense my *fingers* that know this. Recently I used this same machine to introduce my children to touch-typing, and in demonstrating the first exercise to them I had to be aware of which letter each finger covered. I realized immediately that I did not know which letter each finger covered in any communicable way *other than* letting my fingers type words which contained these letters. For if I tried to picture each letter and name it to myself as the exercise required, I could no longer touch-type at all! Undoubtedly at the beginning I, too, consciously matched a letter with each key and with different fingers. But I had long since ceased to do this, and now it is literally my fingers that know how to type whatever I want to express to my readers. The exercise tells the beginner not to look at the keys. I don't have to be told. If I look it takes me longer to find the words I want. Yet my touch-typing is not an unconscious activity, a mindless process. I know exactly what I am doing. And it really makes no difference whether I say I know or my fingers know.

This may not, on reflection, be as good as Merleau-Ponty's examples, but it serves as a caution against premature assumption of a dualism of mind and matter. It also goes some way towards giving content to the mystery of human beings' primordial preconception of this world of which they are so integral a part, and it can even prepare the ground for such Christian themes as the body of Christ moving through the world in the world's history. Thrown-projection involves an incarnate spirit or, even better, an inspired body in a material world which already incorporates something of rationality, of mind or spirit.

## A new view of the relationship between history and faith

Hans Georg Gadamer took from Heidegger this thrown-projection description of human existence and transposed it into another, more accessible, key. 'Thrown-ness' now becomes There-being's belonging to his past, his tradition. He already knows the past, perhaps more than he realizes, because tradition is his context, because he is inset in it. But again, not inertly, rather as project; in Merleau-Ponty's words, 'the project towards the world which we are'. It is in this key that the analysis of human existence offers the clearest guidelines for a larger concept of history, and proves the truth of Heidegger's contention that history is closer to primordial knowing than it is to the more artificial scientific methods which naïve empiricists urge upon us as models for all knowing.

The circle image is now transposed into Gadamer's cognate image of the merging or fusion of horizons. (I say cognate because horizons are circular too.) So, There-being now knows his past, his tradition, perhaps as resistance, in the very process of projecting his future, just as his future is known to him as the past projects through him its as yet unrealized possibilities. Only in this fusion can two different horizons of past and future be known, and simultaneously the essentially historical nature of existence is realized. Neither horizon, not even the horizon of the past, can be known independently, as if it were a datum, a given, lying as yet undetected in the hinterland of our lives.

History, then, is the result of fusing our projects with our inheritance; in the course of this fusion the dialogue occurs which alone enables the past to speak for itself. And it is *within* this circular movement, the hermeneutical circle, as it is called, that the more circumscribed scientific methods are used, for dating things, for establishing the authenticity of texts, for verifying specific hypotheses in quite specific ways. Once the general structure of human knowledge is established, the subsidiary disciplines can find their place and can be of service within this. The danger of any contributory method being elevated by wayward philosophers to the status of sole model for human knowledge is thus averted.

That, then, is the kind of reflection on human existence which supports Heidegger's view that history comes closest to that primordial understanding which most essentially characterizes our human existence in the world. But how does all this help in overcoming the more frequently advertised dichotomy between history and faith? The clue is provided by Merleau-Ponty when he actually names 'primordial faith', that general and most basic structure of human knowledge in which it at once prepossesses and projects. Indeed, if we were not all victims of a late Western cultural chauvinism which instinctively downgrades faith in the course of its bias against religious faith, we should not be in the least surprised at such deep and broad use of the world faith as is now intended.

From the beginnings of Western epistemology the word 'faith' has been used to refer to the most comprehensive range of human knowledge. Aristotle used the word of the premises on which a ratiocinative process was based, *and* of the conclusion reached at the end of that process. In the great Platonic tradition 'faith' referred to the kind of knowledge we have of the spatio-temporal world (what we should now call 'science' in common parlance), but it also came to refer to the highest apprehension of the highest being available to us in this life. Today the claim to rehabilitate the word 'faith' might be better expressed by saying that all knowledge is more or less justified and hence more or less rational belief. In either case it is perfectly possible to sustain the claim of the term 'faith' or 'belief' to name the most comprehensive forms of human knowledge, the most fundamental forms of human understanding, within which the more critically reflective exercises of ratiocination take place. And that is the case for saying that history, understanding, and faith do very greatly coincide. That is the case for questioning the dichotomy between history and faith which has done such damage in philosophical and theological circles to both.

It is always useful to point out to the more naïve empiricists, who are inclined to set scientific knowledge against any kind of faith, that the more immediate the perception the less susceptible it is of verification and the more I have to take it on faith. I must believe that what I see is indeed a blade of grass and not a plastic substitute; only when I go beyond the immediacy of the original perception and do something about this alleged blade of grass can I verify my original faith in the fact that it is a blade of grass. And similar structures of verification can deal with more elaborate forms of human faith.

Now if human knowledge in its primordial and hence its most universal structure can be called faith, surely there can be no dichotomy between history and faith, for history is just that form of knowing which most clearly mirrors the historical nature of existence and the temporality of being. History, the process, is formed by the way in which human beings prepossess their world and their traditions and in and through these project themselves towards an intrinsically uncertain future. History, the discipline, is pursued by those who fashion a project—it might be a 'purely' academic project to gain a Ph.D., or a more 'practical' project such as one might find in economic history or the history of science—in order to interpret that which is already possessed or inherited. Two sides of the same coin, one the inverse image of the other, and both of them very good images, as Heidegger suggested, of that characteristically human way of knowing which Merleau-Ponty actually called 'primordial faith'. And so history, both the process and the discipline, can be described reasonably enough as human faith in action—in the process perhaps more active, in the discipline more critically reflective. Or if 'faith' is felt to be too compromised a word, then recourse could be had to the clumsy phrase 'more or less rational belief' in action. In any case, the dichotomous distinction between faith and history must surely fall.

But we must not rush our fences. The authors who introduced the dichotomy between faith and history may have been thinking, after all, about religious faith in particular, not about some general type of human faith which one might just as easily call rational belief, as in the statement: all human knowledge is really a form of more or less rational belief. It was *religious* faith and history that these authors—Bultmann, Butterfield, Harvey— were keeping quite distinct. In other words, they may not have been denying the general assertion that there are no uninterpreted facts, but merely insisting that *religious* interpretations have always to be brought to and superimposed upon whatever (otherwise interpreted) facts we may find, for *religious* interpretation cannot have the same sort of human origin as other forms of interpretation in which we take up our past. The philosopher, then, the secular prophet, the poet and, of course, the professional historian may forge that hermeneutical circle which is called history, but not the theologian. After all, Heidegger, Gadamer, and Merleau-Ponty all keep *their* distance from religious faith; they can find no place for it within the universal structures of human knowledge. Hence if we use their works in order to counter the dichotomy between faith and history, and to show that faith is a perfectly good word for the kind of primordial human knowing which is most reflectively cultivated as history, we shall still not have gained much ground. We shall not have shown that this primordial human faith has a religious dimension; and so we shall not have shown that history and religious faith can be coincident and not for ever distinct. Only if we can show this can we use for our purposes the dominant insights of Heidegger, Gadamer, and Merleau-Ponty. But can we show this in the face of such impressive incredulity?

## *The particular case of religious faith*

Let us return to our conversation with There-being. We were about to ask him how 'being' got into the conversation. The answer to this question, he says a little hesitantly, centres on death. For a further feature of There-being's unique mode of existence (i.e. understanding) is that he has a unique and characteristic knowledge of death—a knowledge not shared, for instance, by animals. This known death, which is for There-being the concrete shape of nothingness, is the veil through which being appears. Heidegger, the biographer of There-being, who coined that metaphor, the veil of being, described There-being as a being-unto-death, so endemic to There-being is his consciousness of death. There-being explains as follows this new feature of his understanding of the world.

The reflective nature of There-being's consciousness simply means that There-being is always conscious of being conscious, always self-conscious, always conscious of self in the course of being conscious of anything at all. And this consciousness of being conscious of self and of anything else sets a distance between self and things on the one hand, and consciousness of them on the other. There-being thus comes quite naturally upon the idea of the *absence* of self and of things. Through reflective consciousness the negative enters. Consciousness is *not* altogether coincident with that of which it is conscious. That goes for self-consciousness also, for I can talk to myself, and quite frequently I do. Reflective consciousness thus arrives quite inevitably at the possibility of things and of self not being there at all. (Language, incidentally, is also possible because things and self are 'objectified' and so can be signposted, symbolized, talked about.)

Some things must quickly be noted about this awareness of the possibility of not-being, this frightening knowledge of a mysterious, threatening nothingness . . . no-thingness. First, it is inescapably part and parcel of reflective consciousness, which is the kind of consciousness that characterizes human animals. Only by living very determinedly in the full noise and glare of life's discotheque can one ignore its presence, but ignorance, however long sustained, cannot make it go away. Second, although it is itself a kind of indistinct blur on the edge of all vision, human beings, when they do face up to it, tend to focus upon the event of each one's individual death; but death is a focus for it, not its definition. It stalks the living and could well await them on the other side of death, if there be another side of death. Third, and more positively, it gives a particular comprehensiveness and a particular flavour to the concomitant awareness that self and things do yet quite miraculously exist. A particular comprehensiveness because reflective consciousness taints everything of which it is conscious with the awareness of nothingness; in this way it comes upon such comprehensive terms as 'everything', 'world', 'universe' and, above all, 'being'. A particular flavour because the 'being' of which reflective consciousness is thus aware 'through the veil of nothingness' appears so fragile, so transient, and so precious.

So There-being becomes conscious, through the veil of not-being, of being, as the most fundamental aspect of all, the term with the richest and most comprehensive reference. (The verb to be, or not to be, is the most fundamental in any language, so fundamental that some languages, like Hebrew, simply assume it, and some languages, like Irish, have more than one form of it.) There-being's awareness of nothingness—which takes concrete form for him in the awareness of death, in which, as far as he can see, both he and his world simultaneously disappear—and There-being's consequent awareness of being, is all the more acute, he claims, when the structure of understanding as thrown-projection is taken into account. For his consciousness takes the form of projection of his preconception and so it comprises his actions, his evaluations, his creation; in a single expression, his limited freedom. And now the negative enters in the form of the unknown future, the temporal *not*, not yet and perhaps not at all. Anguish is the emotional response to this essential state of There-being's affairs. Not fear, for fear always has a specific object. In his anguish, the existentialist emotion, There-being discovers death, nothingness . . . and being.

On the question of how the B of Being sometimes at the hands of religious authors becomes a capital letter, There-being is more direct. He realizes that simple capitalization of initial letters, like the A in Absolute, can give some people illusions of instant religious faith. He is at pains, therefore, to explain, since Heidegger and not Hegel is his immediate creator, that the being he sees through the veil of nothingness seems always threatened by nothingness, and never more so than when it seems to be the most surprising of graces, something surprisingly there for him and in him, and through him coming to expression. In other words, as being comes to expression through him it always seems to be 'in question'. And that 'question' can, of course, be formulated in words, In fact, the 'question' was formulated for Therebeing by his creator, Heidegger, as follows: why are there essents, why is there anything at all rather than nothing?

Now this is where, and why, Heidegger wants to distance himself from religion, for Heidegger insists that those for whom the Bible, for example, is revelation have the answer to that question before it is asked. Hence it is for them only a pretend question. God is, and He creates everything else. So the question of questioned and questioning being is answered before it is asked: by positing this 'extra' unquestionable Being.

This is a highly philosophical way of saying that, in Heidegger's view, religious people commonly use what they choose to call religious faith for the sorry purpose of suppressing the most elemental consciousness of reality which human beings can have and which is indeed definitive of the human condition. And this misrepresents the whole of reality. For though reflective consciousness is the inevitable source of the awareness of that insidious nothingness which taints everything, it is not, so far as it is aware, the source of that nothingness. If it were the source of nothingness it could conceivably, by a self-injection of some verbally revealed certainty, rid itself and all reality of the fatal disease. Reflective consciousness does taint all it perceives with the awareness of nothingness—it must consider the nonexistence even of God, and that is why final knowledge of God is commonly thought in religious sources to involve hitherto unexperienced states of altered consciousness—but it is convinced without argument that most, if not all, of what it knows is riddled with mortal negatives. It *therefore* expresses the question mark at the heart of all finite being, and does not presume to provide a peremptory answer to a 'question' which itself describes the existential status of all that is existentially in question. If there is an answer for being which is 'in question', it must take the form of new ways of being, and consequently of new ways of experiencing being in praxis.

It is worth noticing, though, that if Heidegger here appears to rule out the possibility of a faith which simply appropriates a divine revelation, and by positing an 'extra' Being suppresses the very question which being itself poses through There-being, he does not thereby rule out all possible forms of religious faith. What he actually says is this:

On the other hand, a faith that does not perpetually expose itself to the possibility of unfaith is no faith but merely a convenience: the believer simply makes up his mind to adhere to the traditional doctrine. This is neither faith nor questioning, but the indifference of those who can busy themselves with everything, sometimes even displaying a keen interest in faith as well as in questioning.[1]

Heidegger is reported to have said at a theological meeting in Marburg that the true task of theology is to seek the language which is capable of calling to faith *and of preserving in faith*. Religious faith is thus not automatically ruled out for There-being; rather is the task laid upon theology of preserving There-being in genuine faith. For There-being lives by faith, and, though he may wish to rule out some prevenient certainties which masquerade as faith, he does not set any a priori limits to the dimensions of faith.

Let us come back once more to the centrality of death, and look at two Greek writers, Aeschylus and Plato. For Plato philosophy, which in its highest form was to bring us to the likeness of God (*homoiosis theou*), was equally a 'learning to die'. Clearly, then, for Plato, through the experience of death (which is, of course, available to There-being through every project of life), through the veil of nothingness, the Being of God was reached. Gadamer, on the other hand, refers to Aeschylus' phrase *pathei mathos* (learning through suffering), but he takes Aeschylus to affirm in the end that what we learn are the limits of human existence, its inescapably historical character, the barrier that separates it from any 'divine' life. Since suffering and its anguish are but heralds of death, what we learn is simply that we must die. (In the ancient Epic of Gilgamesh, when Gilgamesh recognizes death as the real, the last enemy, and goes in search of the food of immortality, he loses it again: what he learns, then, is that he must die, and that is all.) Yet Gadamer is prepared to say that this recognition of the insurpassable limits of our finite existence is in the end a religious recognition, the recognition from which Greek tragedy was born.

In the New Testament the Letter to the Hebrews says that Jesus learned 'obedience' (which in that literature is equivalent to 'faith') from what he suffered, a phrase remarkably similar to that used by Aeschylus. That one phrase surely shows Jesus to have been thrown-project like the rest of us, a man of similar structure of understanding, a being-unto-death, a man of primordial human faith which, on facing suffering and death, inevitably reaches religious depths, as Gadamer recognized, even if it rejects immortality and God. And that is sufficient to leave Jesus open to history, and to leave open also the quest of the historical Jesus as a founder of faith, a pioneer of faith as Hebrews also calls him.

The being that comes to expression in all our language is universal being, a totality of which we have no comprehensive oversight. The being which comes into question in all our projects does indeed carry the sign of the negative through which its all-embracing breadth and depth and height and power and presence is so barely glimpsed. But if we cannot simply say with Hegel, who fathered this kind of thought, that the negative *will* be negated and the grand and final reconciliation in Absolute Spirit achieved, neither can we simply say that as a matter of course the negative *will* ultimately triumph. Either is as much an expression of faith as the other, and each is an expression of religious faith, for atheism is as much a religious faith, albeit in negative mode, as any form of theism. One might, of course, refuse both of these contrasting options and adopt the more rarified, balanced indecision of the agnostic. All that needs to be said at the moment about this third option is that it is relative to forms of religious faith and requires for its establishment the same kind of religious discourse as the other two. And in practice, of course, agnostics like everyone else live by some form of faith. We must see more clearly later that only their deepest practical commitments can show what gods or no-gods people actually believe in; that it is praxis rather than theory that counts.

And what will preserve us in this primordial religious faith, atheistic or otherwise? Simply the theological integrity that can continue to bring to consciousness, at the depths of all our thrown-projections, the being that thus comes to expression through us and moves in space and time, with its question and risk, its promise and hope.

History is the form of knowing which is closest to that understanding which in turn is the characteristic mode of existence of There-being as thrown-projection, and which, at the deepest level of its everyday activity, is a primordial religious faith that can of its very nature oscillate between forms of atheism and forms of theism. That, of course, is a very general statement about history, and since the term history refers to quite a range of intellectual activities, it will prove problematic in different ways depending upon what kind of activity one has in mind at any particular moment. At one end of the range, where certain dating techniques are in use, it will sound excessively philosophical to the point of pomposity. At the other end, where the historian must deal with those deep, comprehensive, and powerfully influential views about reality that are truly religious even if they are sometimes atheistic, it will inevitably encounter the current cultural bias against the metaphysical. But as long as history is pursued by professionals or amateurs who realize that its full range must encompass the totality of the long human effort to understand and to manage this world, the statement will ring true.

On this account of it, then, history can ask and hope to answer the question of the relationship between Jesus and the Christian faith. On this account of it, however, history will also open on to other issues of importance in modern theology. If There-being's *apologia pro vita sua* is in the main acceptable, then is it not impossible for us to begin with a pre-existent divine being who spoke or acted through Jesus, or with any divine being conceived as an 'extra' Being, extra to the being which comes to expression in us, whose 'revelations' are deposited in history? If Jesus was human, if he was There-being too, must we not first approach through the common structures of our primordial religious faith, the common structures which lie at the depth of all our historical projects, and through this try to discern the specific shape of the faith which he pioneered? The answer to that long question, I think, is: yes. We must begin with faith rather than revelation, with the man rather than the God; to get to the roots of the man's significance, we must ignore at first the attraction of titles with their suggestion of circumscribed roles, and go to the man's humanity. If he founded a faith, that can be discovered, and we can also discover what it was. But our historical access must be through the universal structures of human understanding, through our common primordial faith. And since understanding, before any differentiation into the different directions of pragmatic and theoretical interest (as Gadamer would say), is conscious project in body and act, our essential access to the faith of Jesus may also have to be described as bodily and in act.

## Imagination

Modern theology in fact offers another way of approaching the problem of the historical Jesus, and in particular the problem of his relationship to the faith which has ever since claimed him as its founder. This way is through the modern philosophy of imagination, and through cognate areas of study in which imagination is of central significance and religion is also of interest: religion and literature, the study of metaphor and parable, the study of symbol and myth. To many people this way may well prove more attractive than that which lies through the science-fiction landscape of There-being, signposted in his unfamiliar jargon, yet it is remarkable how similar are the features of these two ways, and how they provide a similar sort of access to similar areas of modern theological debate. So similar are their main features that one might be tempted to think that they were in fact the same way seen through different cultural spectacles. In any case, it is worth describing the way of imagination before ending this chapter.

It is first necessary to rescue imagination from its imprisonment in the age-old prejudice that it is the faculty of the childish and the fanciful, wilful, wild, and at times demoniacally destructive. Hence the value of Mary Warnock's book on *Imagination*, in which she demonstrates with the aid of established philosophers of the modern era, the essential role played by imagination in all ordinary knowing. So successful is the demonstration that imagination should now take its place alongside other terms which also embrace the complex unity of our conscious presence in the world and cover a wide range of analytically distinguished mental activities. The rehabilitation of imagination places it in company with such terms as reason, experience, and understanding, and this is the first of the features to remind us of Therebeing's more esoteric account of his peculiar mode of existence. Other more specific similarities follow. For nothing illustrates as well as imagination that preconception or prepossession of reality of which There-being spoke.

The impressions of the world which we receive are not discrete and serial, patches of colour accompanied by various sounds and other miscellaneous sensations, all perceived in an atomic series of present moments, nor are such series of atomic impressions 'later' organized by some mental faculty in terms of time and space and logic. Rather is the world perceived as already organized into continuously existing and interrelated objects which we can then name, analyse, and investigate. We can perceive any thing, or part or aspect of a thing, only because we simultaneously, mysteriously, construe in image a 'world', however large or small, in which we live and move and have our being. Images *are* our perceptions of things which always extend beyond the limits of immediate impression and attention. Hence imagination comprises, on the one hand, what we call memory, and on the other, foresight (as There-being might call it), which can blossom into a vision for the future, a value, if I feel bound to it, an ideal. Imagination is necessary, as Mary Warnock says, to enable us to recognize things in the world as familiar, to take for granted features of the world which we need to take for granted and rely on (this involves memory) if we are to go about our ordinary business (this refers to our projects).

In a recent television interview Edna O'Brien was asked yet again about the paradox of so many Irish writers who continue to write about Ireland, and indeed only about Ireland, though they could no longer live in a country that, like an old sow, as Joyce once said, eats its own farrow. She answered by claiming that Ireland was perfectly preserved in the artist's mind. What she was surely implying was that the fine details of its sights and sounds, its mind-sets and landscapes, its subtle tones and the ebb and flow of its feelings, were truer in her imagination than in the minds of many who had stayed. *Of course*, one might say, but that is the artist's preservation, the artist's memory. What has that to do with ordinary memory? Edna O'Brien's *The Country Girls* is not history, is it?

Well, is it? The least that may be said is that it is imagination that knows the past as past by its ability to represent it in image. The most that may be said is that it is those who lack artistic perception who fail to see the revelations of reality, and lock it instead into dead symbols and heavily mortgaged categories. Imagination, in Wallace Stevens' words, though 'one of us', is the necessary angel of earth since, as the angel says,

> In my sight, you see the earth again,
>
> Cleared of its stiff and stubborn, man-locked set,
> And, in my hearing, you hear its tragic drone
> Rise liquidly in liquid lingerings,
> Like watery words awash, like meanings said
> By repetition of half-meanings.
>
> ('Angel Surrounded by Paysans')[2]

Certainly the perception of the poet and the visionary is creative; it does perceive the tragedy of beauty struggling in the ugliness of things, and it is therefore by its nature as much engaged with promise and with hope as it is with anything that could more flatly be called fact. But to say that is to say no more than that the creative artist heightens for us the intrinsic quality of all perception. It is to say again what There-being said, that reality is revealed through the veil of the negative and that our mysterious preconceptions of it are always fused with our projects, and that we can only distinguish preconception and project at all by reflection on this very fusion.

Whatever the historian comes across in the course of his work is, after all, a human creation, and only creative vision, however elementary, can enable it to be understood. Yet of course history can claim to be a science, or at least scientific. Kant attributed to imagination that 'reflective judgement' by which a scientist envisages 'the finality of nature', a pattern or order, that is to say, more far-reaching than any as yet perceived. And within this imaginative activity occur those more nearly physical methods and techniques, those probings and measurings, which are too often taken to provide the single model not only for all science, but for all knowing.

I say 'more nearly physical' rather than simply 'physical' (from 'physics') because I want to avoid at all times those crippling dualities of mental/physical, spiritual/bodily, and although the language does not allow me to operate with single words rather than pairs, and hyphenated words betray their own intention, I want to remember how physical is every spiritual act I know, and how spiritual every physical act I perform. But if I should forget this lesson nothing could more powerfully remind me of it than that work of literary art, Marcel Proust's *A La Recherche du temps perdu*, the novel, the 'fiction', about the way in which we gather up time and arrive at significance. And how bodily it all is, from the very opening pages. Mary Warnock, in her chapter in *Religious Imagination*, refers to Proust's belief at one stage that he had finally lost his creative power and with it, significantly, his 'joy'. Then, on forcing himself to go to a party, he set his foot on uneven paving stones outside the Guermantes' door. A gentle push, and memory opened its gates, on to Venice and a similar pair of uneven stones which his feet had felt in the baptistry of St Mark's, and on to the rising lagoon of sensations and emotions he had then experienced. He was instantly reassured. Joy returned through the most physical of impressions and with it—for these are inseparable—the creative power of imagination which penetrates to the timeless heart of things through the most fleeting of epiphanies.

Another way of realizing how very bodily, how physically engaged, how active is imagination, despite its 'unreal' image, is to recognize with philosophers as staid as Hume and with poets as profound as Wordsworth imagination's endemic quality of engaging the most effective of human emotions, particularly love and fear, respectively the most constructive and the most destructive of these. Wordsworth attributed 'to fear and love' the ability to see things as participatory symbols in the depths of all reality, 'To love as prime and chief, for there fear ends'. And he adds:

> This spiritual love acts not nor can exist
> Without Imagination, which, in truth,
> Is but another name for absolute power
> And clearest insight, amplitude of mind,
> And Reason in her most exalted mood.

('The Prelude')

Contemporary epistemology of imagination, then, is beginning to lead by a gentler path to an apreciation of the basic structures of characteristically human knowing-and-being in this world: its fusion of mysterious prepossession with projection, of perception with emotion and action, its bodiliness, and above all, its function as the matrix within which the more circumscribed and 'exact' sciences make their essential contribution; its intriguing resemblance to history.

But can the word 'faith' be used of imagination, or of its works and products, and is there any justification at all for speaking of religious faith in this connection? The answer to the first part of this question is found partly in the range of activity which imagination covers and entails: from the most basic perception of all starting-points to the envisaging of the most advanced results, from emotional involvement, through personal evaluation, to the most sustained of active commitment (Heidegger's 'preserving in faith'). All this is highly reminiscent of the range of the word 'faith' in traditional Western epistemology, and reminiscent also of Merleau-Ponty's 'primordial faith', of the world of 'the unreflective light of consciousness' as it exists before the

more analytic reflection breaks it up into perception and interpretation, emotion, will and act.

But there is a better reason why faith should be coupled with
imagination. By contrast with the assertions of more didactic
reason, with the apodictic certainties which philosophers since
Descartes seem to have sought, with the measured probabilities
of empiricists, and with the more ancient certainties which speculative theology has come to call dogmas, imagination in its
artistry seeks to enchant rather than to coerce, to haunt rather
than to conclude, to tug at the heart rather than beat about the
head. There is, in short, a delicately tentative, if also a tenacious,
quality about the assent which imagination elicits, and it is a good
deal closer to human faith than anything that any comparable
term might name.

On *religious* faith and imagination little need be said beyond
repeating the point that religious faith is but the highest or
deepest form of human faith and not another kind of faith altogether. Similarly imagination is religious once its vision is sufficiently comprehensive, even if it is the imagination of a
profoundly mystical nihilist like Samuel Beckett. For the rest,
religious imagination has been accorded full recognition, if only
more recently in European thought, by both philosophers and
theologians. Kant talked of 'aesthetic ideas', which were comparable to his ideas of reason in that they dealt with the religious
realm and were in consequence quite beyond the bounds of conceptual thought, and his century is filled with analysis of the sub-
lime, that is to say, that which we seem to encounter alike in the
more awe-inspiring of natural phenomena and in works of artistic genius. Only more recently still has Christian theology come to
grips with the imagery, the metaphor, the symbol, the myth and
drama so prevalent in its own sources, but the lateness of its
arrival on this particular scene promises to be well compensated
for by the sheer volume of its production.

'Christ's place indeed is with the poets', wrote Oscar Wilde in
his *De Profundis* (a marvellous autobiographical account, it may
be said, of learning something of the faith of Jesus through suffering). 'His whole conception of humanity sprang right out of
the imagination and can only be realised by it.'[3] The ancient

religious drama of the meal and the art of parable-telling were Jesus' means of giving people an experience of God's reign, as he called it. He taught no doctrines, added no dogmas, promulgated neither creed nor moral code, and never seemed interested in acting the constitutional lawyer, describing structures, offices, and the protocol of succession. And because Jesus' own faith took the form of an act of historical imagination, it is through an act of historical imagination that we can gain access to it. Like speaks to like.

*     *     *

There is a key, then, to the main theological problem of today, the relationship between Jesus and the Christian religion. It takes the form of the primordial faith of Heidegger's There-being, at least in the shape of the fusion of historical horizons which Gadamer gave it. More simply, it takes the form of an act of historical imagination.

This proves also to be something of a master-key to many subsidiary problems of modern theology. First, a key to the God-problem, as has already been hinted. The poets, too, suggest that the object of religious faith is not to be considered, in Yeats' measured words, 'distant and therefore intellectually understandable'. Rather must we learn to see '*under* the boughs of love and hate/*in* all poor foolish things that live a day/Eternal Beauty wandering on her way' (the italics are mine: Yeats did not need them).[4] It is those who try to prove God's existence, or disprove it, as the existence of a distinct, almost an extra Being, that Sartre's words really impugn: 'even if God did exist, that would change nothing'.[5] But Jesus, we may see, was less a victim of such clear dividing lines between the divine and the human—lines which have often, paradoxically, marred so many later doctrines about Jesus himself. His concern was with the power within, amongst us. The age-old and forever renewed distinction between sacred and secular thus remains threatened by the integrity of his vision.

A key to a great many ecclesiastical problems. Warned by Butterfield about ecclesiastical interpretations of history, we may be able to reject or at least to reduce in significance much that organized bodies have done, and are still doing, in Jesus' name, without thereby being driven to some purely spiritual image of the Christian faith. The action, the drama, the sheer bodiliness of the Thing, as Chesterton called it, not only survives but in fact supports such ecclesiastical critique. Spiritual/bodily and all cognate dichotomies are but further evasions of this uniquely human and historical vision.

A key to the problem of faith and history, but enough has been said about this. And, perhaps, that the faith/history dichotomy is in one way merely another version of the spirit/body dichotomy elongated in time. And that a dissolution of that dichotomy of faith and history provides the final solution to the problem of the nature of divine revelation; a problem which was very much discussed in recent theology, until it was finally suggested that revelation was history. Now if revelation takes the form of history and history is human faith in action, then it follows that the faith of Jesus, and the faith he inspires in his followers, is for Christians the oldest and deepest relevation of the divine. But this point about divine revelation can only become clear when the essential dimension of praxis is added to this account of faith.

And last, a key that allows us to bypass for the moment the many titles of Jesus, ancient and modern, each encapsulating its own circumscribed version of the problem of the quest for the historical Jesus, so that we can arrive directly at Jesus the man.

# 2

# The Way (i)

'The philosophers have only interpreted the world in various ways; the point is to change it.' This is the last and best known of Marx's *Theses On Feuerbach*. It seems worth quoting yet again at this point because it introduces one of the few great contributions made by philosophy since the seventeenth century, a contribution, moreover, which has been largely monopolized by atheistic humanists and used extensively in the modern critique of Christianity. It has to do with the role of practice in the very process of human understanding, with the 'doing' that it is maintained is inevitably involved with all true and false knowing, and with the equally inevitable social dimension of what is then described as praxis, a word of Greek origin which connotes knowledgeable practice or practised knowledge.

There-being's account of basic human understanding already included the element of perceiving, the element of evaluating, and the creative element, all in a kind of pre-analytic or primordial unity. The philosophy of imagination, once it had made clear that imagination is indeed an extremely comprehensive word for our ways of knowing and not, as in some old faculty psychology, the name of a supernumerary psychic ability of quite doubtful use in the quest for truth, went further and illustrated the central place held in our imaginative processes by the most powerful of human emotions, love and fear. These emotions are the springs of all human action, respectively of the most constructive and the most destructive of human action, so praxis was never in fact far from view. Imagination of its very nature enlists the power of the concrete, particularly the power to reveal and to inspire, so it is rightly seen as that which gives access to the life of Jesus in his time and in ours. But it seems right, in view of the thrust of modern philosophy after Hegel, to highlight still further the practical features of human understanding and, in view of the atheistic direction of this thrust, to ask even more pointedly if we must satisfy ourselves with a human life, perhaps in some respects like the life of Jesus, but without faith in God.

## Humanist praxis

The credit for drawing attention to the role of doing in the quest for truth does not belong entirely to Feuerbach and Marx. American pragmatism made the case in its own independent manner. Nearer home, in a provocative and original presidential address to the Aristotelian Society (1945–6), Gilbert Ryle claimed that 'knowledge-how is a concept prior to knowledge-that'—for even a scientist is primarily a man who knows *how* to decide certain sorts of question. Ryle in this way sought to make plain the central role of human conduct in the process of arriving at a knowledge of reality, and to combat the more accepted view that a body of theoretical knowledge had somehow to be already in place before human conduct could be considered rational or, further still, moral or even artistic. Perhaps he erred in reversing too completely the conventional priorities, in thinking knowledge-how logically prior to knowledge-that, in believing conduct, doing, logically prior to accumulation of known 'principles' or 'facts'. Perhaps it is better to see all knowledge as requiring, at every stage and simultaneously, a capacity to do and a capacity to recognize, and to regard these as twin aspects of one and the same process of human understanding, the latter having been emphasized traditionally at the expense of the former. Of course Aristotle long ago preached the necessity of practical experience in the pursuit of moral wisdom, and Bacon showed the way for experiment in science, but it was not until the modern period that the analysis of the role of doing in all areas of knowledge and understanding began, and it is still very far from complete. It is, however, well enough advanced to add its own insights to Therebeing's self-description as thrown-project, and to imagination's claim to be the most comprehensive term for human ways to the truth.

Further, since it reveals the process of understanding to be a veritable complex of active relationships, embodied mind acting and reacting with the rest of reality, the modern practicalist thesis, as it has been called, opens more easily than conventional views upon the inherently social character of the pursuit of truth, goodness, and beauty. And it is this feature of the practicalist thesis that must focus attention upon the forms it was given by the followers of Hegel, particularly Feuerbach and Marx, however much we may also have to learn from some British and American philosophers. In fact Feuerbach and Marx have a further claim upon our attention in that they use the practicalist thesis in its full social and historical dimension to persuade us that the kernel of truth in Christianity is to be found in humanism, in human action for humanity's own goals. The unqualified acceptance of the full and undiminished humanity of Jesus meant, for Feuerbach at least, that man was indeed man's own and only God.

## Hegel's universe

Hegel was, of course, the great immanentist, rivalled only by the earliest Stoa in his determination to see both God and man at home together in this universe. His purpose from the very first page of his philosophy to the last was profoundly religious. His aim was 'to embrace the whole energy of the suffering and discord that has controlled the world and all forms of its culture, and also to rise above it'. But 'above it' did not refer to any world other than the one we now know, and so he sought 'a new religion in which the infinite grief and the whole gravity of its discord is acknowledged, but is at the same time serenely and purely dissolved'.[1] The riddle of the identity of Hegel's God has puzzled many a student, and the attempt to decide whether it was or was not, as Hegel himself thought, the Christian God, still keeps a mini-industry going.

In a sense the question has broadened beyond the ranks of Hegelian exegetes. For, with some insular exceptions, if one might reapply some words of Whitehead's, all modern Western philosophy is a series of footnotes to Hegel. And since theology has never quite been able to ignore philosophical fashion—even Karl Barth's unilateral declaration of independence has not saved him from the suggestion that in all his own theology he makes implicit use of Kantian epistemology and metaphysics—modern theology, too, is more beholden to Hegel than many of its practitioners are prepared to admit. And so the question about Hegel's God inevitably broadens into the question: did the immanentist thrust of Hegel's philosophy find its truest expression in the philosophies of Feuerbach and Marx, or must these be classed as aberrations, and does modern Christian theology still have to pursue the quest for a vision of *the Christian truth of this world* to which Hegel in his powerful way tried to recall it?

In general, left-wing students and followers of Hegel felt that the Master had leant too far towards mind or spirit, and that he had thus too easily assumed that the discord in the world could be serenely dissolved by understanding and reason, that it was in fact dissolved already, if only in principle in his own mind, in terms of the phenomenology of spirit he had produced. Philosophically stated, these misgivings meant that Hegel's more radical followers felt that thought was once more displacing concrete reality; theologically stated, that for Hegel mind or spirit was still the one subject of which all worldly action and success should be predicated—in which case the immanence of the divine in the world conferred as much status on worldlings as Gulliver's presence in Liliput conferred upon the Liliputians.

However fair or unfair all this may have been to Hegel, it is a simple historical fact that the most influential of his immediate followers placed all the emphasis upon the practical struggle of finite agents to bring into the world the truth, freedom, and justice, and the end of grief and discord, which the Master had so powerfully previewed. Human praxis was to regain the centre of the stage on which the cosmic drama was played; we were to dispense with the *deus ex machina*.

### Feuerbach's denial of a transcendent God

Feuerbach's version of this criticism of Hegel is perhaps the best known. His book *The Essence of Christianity* found immediate and widespread popularity and attracted as its English translator one of the greatest of English prose-writers, George Eliot. But it was at the beginning of his slightly more pompously named *Preliminary Theses for the Reform of Philosophy* (1843) that

Feuerbach stated most succinctly the point of his disagreement with Hegel: the secret of speculative philosophy (i.e. Hegel's philosophy) was still theology, he maintained, but the secret of theology was anthropology. Anthropology is here to be taken in its continental European sense—the whole study of man, of the essential features of human nature and of its furthest prospects— and the point of Feuerbach's remark is this: God was still secreted within Hegel's philosophy as the real subject of world history, but if the truth were to be told man has been secreted within all religions as the real subject of their myths and epics, and with Christianity at last the secret was out.

We should not, as is the case in theology and speculative philosophy, make real beings and things into arbitrary signs, vehicles, symbols, or predicates of a distinct, transcendent absolute, i.e., an abstract being; but we should accept and understand them in the significance which they have themselves . . . thus only do we obtain the key to a real theory and practice.

So Feuerbach wrote in the introduction to *The Essence of Christianity*. This is a deliberate onslaught upon the religious imagination, upon its pretensions, in Mary Warnock's words, 'to see the world as significant of something unfamiliar . . . to treat the objects of perception as symbolizing or suggesting things other than themselves'.[2] Man, according to Feuerbach, is not made in the image of a distant God. The highest human qualities of goodness and creativity, freedom and justice, are not poor reflected images of absolute values already secure in some timeless transcendence. Bread is not a symbol of the presence of the Wholly Other; wine is simply good for the stomach and gladdening to the heart, and those who drink it need no further justification. However one analyses human nature—say man is made up of reason, will, and affection—one is bound to discover that in all the known universe man is the great For-Itself. Reason knows for the sake of knowing, will loves for the sake of loving, and joy is its own reward. Even the gods are put there to save us from evil and to guarantee our prospects of eternal well-being. In the most apparently self-denying of his beliefs, man still has only human ends in view.

Feuerbach was well aware of the fact that the adjective 'atheist' was used by religious people to designate those who refused to worship their particular God. Just as early Christians were called atheists by their first cultured despisers, so modern Christians, who still fail to see the real point of their own religion in which a man is worshipped, will in their turn call Feuerbach an atheist. But he must protest at this. 'He alone is the true atheist,' he insists, 'to whom the predicates of the Divine Being—for example, love, wisdom, justice—are nothing.'[3] And he adds: 'What today is atheism, tomorrow will be religion',[4] as it was in the beginning with Christianity. For the pursuit and the achievement of these limitless, infinite values—love, wisdom, justice—is the proper business of man. Man is their true subject, they are human predicates. Those who deny such values are atheists, those who worship their final incarnation in the whole human race have arrived at last at the secret of religion and the essence of Christianity.

It is naturally not easy to test the validity of this Promethean project. The dangers of attributing to human beings total autonomy in the creation of human values are obvious. Religion, with its claims and counter-claims, is all too frequently divisive; it frequently sucks the life out of human love, the truest and noblest of our emotions, by insisting that we love only God and love our fellows only for God's sake and for God's purposes, and it can engender long-sighted selfishness in the service of an ultimately selfish God. All this must be granted Feuerbach; it has always been too obvious to deny. But human groups, even single individuals, have caused inestimable suffering by imposing upon the world, or by seeking to do so, the shape of truth and the form of justice which they have decided is best for us all. What is to be our protection against such recurrent human arbitrariness, when all the other gods have gone? This question is still one of the most pressing to an age whose mood Feuerbach read so well.

Feuerbach answers the question in two ways. First, he suggests that the true subject of the divine predicates is the human species, not any particular group or individual, and not even any particular segment of the species which exists at any particular time. Truth and justice, and all the other values in perfect form, are attributes of humanity itself. Second, human autonomy with respect to these values must not be taken to mean that the human will quite arbitrarily decides upon the content of each. And here the materialism of Feuerbach comes into play, that is to say, his insistence that the beings and things in this world derive their significance from what they are in themselves and not as symbols of some transcendent absolute. Human nature has an empirical content, it has describable needs and processes. The same is true of the other things and beings which share its world with it. Humanity will find its ultimate truth and justice, and whatever other values it may know, by respecting the given needs and processes of the community of beings in the only world it knows.

These are very good answers as far as they go. The concrete nature of human need is given a pivotal position in the argument, and in the total context of Feuerbach's thought even that apparently ineradicable human need which Mephistopheles called 'the cruel thirst for worship' finds its place. The human species, all its needs fulfilled and all its values realized, the whole species and not any particular person or period, is the new deity.

Yet further and more pointed questions must now arise. How are we to think of this total humanity, this species-being as Feuerbach called it, which is subject of all fulfilling action and of all predicates of perfection? Is it the sum total of all individual human beings and peoples, assuming that history should ever allow us to arrive at a total? And is the perfection in question the sum of all good over all evil, assuming that the former is the larger? Or is the reference rather to some state and age of humanity yet to come when all tears will by human endeavour be wiped away? And in either case what is the place of suffering past and present? Are those who die too soon or too cruelly simply an accidental waste product, or the product of a process which has not yet come to the point of efficiency at which it can eliminate such waste? And again, in *either* case, what does this humanity, this species-being, do for its individual tragedies?

By making a species-being the true subject of history one avoids the need to endorse the destructive Fuehrers, but does one also lose the opportunity to say anything worthwhile to the individual failures? Feuerbach had, after all, criticized traditional religion for proposing a distinct, transcendent absolute, in other words an abstract being, to the humiliation and oppression of so many people, and religion will have to answer to that very substantial charge. But it is surely one of the ironies of recent history, which some no doubt find quite delicious, that Marx should have described Feuerbach's view of human nature in language that was both reminiscent of Feuerbach's own and equally dismissive, as 'an abstract being squatting outside the world'.[5] Engels, too, who described the Christian God as 'the product of a tedious process of abstraction',[6] accused Feuerbach of making equally abstract the values which he tried to take back from the Christian God in order to return them to man's species-being. What, one might well ask, is happening here in this far from arid philosophical debate?

Feuerbach was surely correct in castigating the religious imagination of his time for failing to envisage a truly salvific divine presence in the things and beings of this world; he thought that religion treated the latter as arbitrary signs or symbols of a separate abstract being, such that the service of this being largely impoverished human kind. Abstract beings squatting outside the world are something of a menace in any case, the more so the more perfect and powerful they are thought to be. But Feuerbach failed when it came to the more positive part of his task: to envisage the truly salvific subject, or interrelated subjects, and the kind of praxis in this world which could promise something better. At that point his own imagination flagged and failed him, and he too substituted abstractions for the practical, healing vision.

Marx thanked him for his demolition work, took from him his term 'species-being', and set about the construction of a truer vision of this species-being in concrete action which would change for the better the whole face of the earth. But two questions must be put to Marx: first, does his own work meet the practicalist criterion which Feuerbach's failed to meet; and, second, can Marx's vision find a positive place for the suffering of past and present, for what Hegel once called 'patience and the labour of the negative'? On the answer to that particular question the case for all comprehensive visions is likely to rest, whether they call themselves religious visions or not.

## Marx's Practicalist Thesis

The second of Marx's *Theses on Feuerbach* reads as follows:

The question whether objective truth can be attributed to human thinking is not a question of theory but is a practical question. Man must
prove the truth, i.e. the reality and power, the this-sidedness of his
thinking in practice. The dispute over the reality or non-reality of thinking that is isolated from practice is a purely scholastic question.[7]

Seldom, if ever, has the practicalist thesis been quite so boldly
stated. But does Marx's own philosophical work match up to the
requirements of this thesis? An answer to this question, if an
acceptable one could be given, would surely at one and the same
time support his self-proclaimed superiority over Feuerbach and
help people to find, amongst the many versions of Marxism
which clamour for attention, the kind of concrete dream—like
Adam's dream in Milton—which best represents the man himself. For if the thought of Marx, crystallized now in the large
corpus of his extant works, is to be taken as an abstract description of human nature, its characteristic attributes and activities,
and no more, then he is in fact no better than Feuerbach, however different his definition of human nature might be.

'The chief defect of all hitherto existing materialism (that of
Feuerbach included)', so states the first of the *Theses on
Feuerbach*, 'is that the thing, reality, sensuousness, is conceived
only in the form of the object or of contemplation, but not as
sensuous human activity, as practice, not subjectively.' Hegel
had made spirit the subject of history, had talked of spirit taking
the alien form of object (rather than subject) in the material
universe, and had a proleptic experience of the grand reconciliation, the great at-one-ment; but as far as Marx was concerned
Hegel had achieved this reconciliation only in the mind. The
complaint of abstraction could therefore be hurled, for in the end
this reconciliation was abstracted from the world of toil and
struggle in which people, whether they like it or not, have to take
action. Feuerbach felt that the real trouble with Hegel was the
similarity of his system to those traditional Christian positions in
which the divine subject of history was an absolute being quite
above and beyond the world and quite distinct from its struggles.

Turning Hegel on his head, so to say, Feuerbach suggested that it was concrete human subjects who objectified their nature and spirit in the alien form of absolute spirit and thus created the distinct absolute; all would be well once these humans realized that it was their own very worldly species-being that they had projected on to absolute spirit, and once they recognized again, no longer by means of this detour, their own nature.

As far as Marx was concerned, the first part of this was true—people do get the gods they want, and more often than not the gods they deserve, by abstracting from their experience the concepts to which they direct worship—but the second part, in Feuerbach's account of human nature was fatally flawed. It remained, therefore, a half-truth which subverted the whole truth, as all half-truths tend to do. For Feuerbach still construed his concepts of this-worldly, this-sided human nature in terms too much abstracted from *what people do*. For Marx, as he put it in the sixth of his *Theses on Feuerbach*, human nature is not 'an internal, dumb generality which naturally unites the many individuals', it is, rather, 'the ensemble of the social relations'. The problem is, of course, as many a sociological treatise quite amply proves, that an ensemble of the social relations can be described as abstractly as anything else. And if the description should offer a set of solutions by which problems in this ensemble might be overcome, these too could surely be dismissed as solutions in the mind only, as theory abstracted from the concrete struggle, as the work of philosophers still interpreting the world and still failing to change it.

It is not enough to answer: yes, but the social relations which Marx has in mind actually consist of sets of actions and reactions which make the individuals engaged in these what at any time they are. Feuerbach, if he could have answered Marx, could have claimed as much for the values which he won back for human beings from an empty heaven. Justice, he could have said, consists of sets of actions and reactions, and these actions can be described in ever more detail as my humanist philosophy is further developed. Yet, according to Marx, the difference between himself and Feuerbach (and Hegel also) is not the difference between rival theories, one of which may be thought to be right in those respects in which the other is thought to be wrong. The difference, for Marx, is that Feuerbach remained in the abstract, whereas he succeeded in making the transition to the subjective apprehension of reality 'as sensuous human activity', to the knowing-how that is at every stage essential to knowing-that.

Marx, with an insistence that would rival Sartre, presents man as the creator of his own life. Not, of course, in splendid isolation. The material world, to borrow Marx's own language, is man's inorganic body, and so his creative work, his labour, in which his whole freedom and dignity consists, is a working over, a practical creation of a whole objective world. It is in his *doing*, then, that man makes himself a real object, as he creates his life on the visible stage of history; not in the ways that Hegel or Feuerbach thought. And it is in this doing, this *practical* way of objectifying human nature, and in this way creating a human world, that things have up to this point gone wrong. Marx does not, however, explain this wrong by reference to a distant golden age and a fall. It is the theologian, he wrote rather tartly, who explains the origin of evil in terms of the fall, that is to say, he presupposes as a historical fact what he should be explaining. For Marx it is more than enough to begin where he finds us and to analyse our fallen state in terms of alienated labour and private property or, to put it more tersely, in terms of 'the connection of all this alienation with the money system'.

## Marx on alienation

In our current system of self- and world-creation everything that I produce is a commodity. Oxford University Press will give me a few hundred pounds for this manuscript and a small percentage of the money it makes from marketing the book. I lecture at the University of Edinburgh of course, but since the present Prime Minister does not consider theologians to be amongst the creators of wealth (by which she means money), who knows how long that will last? Every product of my labour is a commodity, an object of exchange in the market-place where the medium of exchange is money. Everything that matters is therefore privately owned by those who can afford it. So if I am to feed, clothe, and shelter myself, I have to produce commodities and exchange them through the medium of money for the necessities of life.

I do not create my life by my labour; much less do I co-create a world with others. Instead I produce commodities in order to live, and my life, from the question of its quality down to the point of mere subsistence, is at the mercy of the profit motive, the movement of money. This book should be my expression of my nature and, in so far as it might meet one of your needs, an expression of our communal nature as co-creators of a better world; it is instead a commodity which I have exchanged for my means of livelihood and for which you will exchange something in turn, if you have something to exchange for it. Instead of remaining an expression of myself it has become an object, *alienus*, another thing, alien. I have become alienated from the product of my labour, and since the product is the result of my labour, I have become alienated from my labour also. It also is a commodity. And once these two are seen as commodities, once their value, indeed their nature, is expressed in terms of the exchange medium, money, then everything follows which unfolds in Marx's story. The more I produce the less there is of me. 'It is just the same in religion,' wrote Marx. 'The more man puts into God, the less he retains in himself. The worker puts his life into the object and this means that it no longer belongs to him but to the object.'[8] It can come to the point, Marx warned, where only in eating, drinking and procreating (though we should now probably substitute plain sex), and perhaps in style of dress or dwelling place, can people freely express themselves, and thus they are reduced to the status of animals. Not that eating and drinking and sex are animal as opposed to human activities; only when they are separated from all that would make us communally human, and so forced to be ends in themselves, do they resemble the similar functions of animals, but without the safeguards of animal instinct. The alienation in fact goes deeper still and affects our very sense of being 'at home' with what is potentially the most self-fulfilling of our activities: 'He is at home,' wrote Marx of the worker, 'when he is not working and when he works he is not at home.'[9]

So neither my labour nor its product is any longer my self-expression, my self-creation. Both are mere commodities; their value, even their nature better expressed in terms of their exchange rates, in terms of money. Worse still, this alienation of myself from my labour and its product entails also my alienation from my fellow human beings, and from nature. I have created an object that comes between me and other human beings, because it is not my self-presentation for them, nor, as would be the case if it simply answered to one of their needs, is it their self-presentation to me. It comes between us, between any one of us and any other, preventing direct personal relationships, forging only impersonal relationships which depend upon the market value of what we each privately possess. You can buy my book or hear my lecture if you can pay for it; I can publish my book or give my lecture if I can sell them to someone. I am also, therefore, a commodity, and so are you, worth so much in market terms. Our relationships are regulated not by ourselves but by private property or, to put it more simply, by money, since money is the common or abstract essence of private property.

And nature? Our inorganic body? It is the body in which we, like all the animal species, create our lives. But animal species lack reflective consciousness and so they simply adapt the accessible parts of nature to their immediate needs. We, however, are reflectively conscious of ourselves, of our activities, and of the nature in which we act. We are, in short, self-conscious. Through such consciousness, as we have seen, nothingness enters the world. But the positive side of this reflective consciousness is that we are conscious of totalities, of our whole species and our whole universe. As Heidegger said, we see being through the veil of nothingness; or, as Schleiermacher put it, we come upon the concept of *world* through the immediate self-consciousness of absolute dependence. That is to say: the common bond of finite being, of the only kind of being we can directly know, is its finiteness, its contingency, its might-just-as-well-not-be status, its state of dependency.

So we perceive totalities like world, universe, being, through the veil of nothingness, the sense of absolute and questioning dependence. But we *do* perceive these totalities, and it is thus of the very nature of human consciousness to be 'grandly related' to all, as much in our *praxis* as in our *theoria*. Somewhere in the dark recesses of our consciousness we know that our fate is bound up with that of all finite being and we may even be permitted to suspect, without pride, that its fate too is bound up with ours—the whole world groaning for the liberation of the 'sons of God', as Paul once put it. Self-conscious creation is therefore, or should be, creation by the whole human species, knowing and respecting the inner harmonies of the other species of animal and thing, the inner harmony of all nature. As Marx said: 'man knows how to produce according to the measure of every species and knows everywhere how to apply its inherent standard to the object; thus man also fashions things according to the laws of beauty.'[10]

Or does he? If he acted in accordance with the deepest communal structures of his self-consciousness and the universal dimensions of his understanding, then he would create ever greater harmony and beauty. But in fact he creates by alienated labour alien products to be appropriated as private property, and nature itself becomes a mere supplier of raw material to be rated according to the movements of the market-place. In short, nature, too, is now a commodity and its value is determined financially. It, too, joins the alien objective forces which we have created in such a way that they rule our lives, as a master rules his slaves.

I have tried to create some concrete impression of what Marx means by human alienation in its fourfold dimension: alienation from the product of my labour, from my labour which creates our life and our world, from humanity, and from nature. I am acutely aware of the fact that my efforts are entirely lacking in the power and precision of Marx's own analysis, for example, in the sections on alienated labour in the *Economic and Philosophical Manuscripts*. But I hope that they are nevertheless sufficient to serve the following dual purpose: to set in relief Marx's positive vision of what a truly human world created by truly human labour would look like, and by this route to return to the original question about Marx's own philosophical output *vis-à-vis* his rather strident claims about praxis. First, then, to the vision. Like most men who have tried to envisage the eschaton, Marx also exercised a great deal of very necessary reserve. So it is perhaps

worth quoting in full one of the few passages in which he goes
into any detail.

Supposing that we had produced in a human manner, each of us would
in his production have doubly affirmed himself and his fellow men. I
would have: (1) objectified in my production my individuality and its
peculiarity and thus both in my activity enjoyed an individual expression
of my life and also in looking at the object have had the individual
pleasure of realizing that my personality was objective, visible to the
senses and thus a power raised beyond all doubt. (2) In your enjoyment
or use of my product I would have had the direct enjoyment of realizing
that I had both satisfied a human need by my work and also objectified
the human essence and therefore fashioned for another human being the
object that met his need. (3) I would have been for you the mediator
between you and the species and thus been acknowledged and felt by you
as a completion of your own essence and a necessary part of yourself and
have thus realized that I am confirmed both in your thought and in your
love. (4) In my expression of my life I would have fashioned your expression of your life, and thus in my own activity have realized my own
essence, my human, my communal essence.

In that case our products would be like so many mirrors, out of which
our essence shone.[11]

It is difficult to expand upon the vision without in fact less-
ening it. It is clear that Marx can see how we could take up nature
into our self-creating and world-creating processes (our labour)
in such a way that we could really create our human selves in true
communion of action and reception, rather than expending ourselves and our natural world in search of products which merely
set us apart and in competition with each other, getting and
spending and laying waste our powers until nothing indeed is left
of nature that is ours. It is equally clear that, however much he
may analyse the self-destructive logic of capitalism by which the
end of the present age of inhumanity is ushered in, Marx cannot
come up with such detail of the new age as to satisfy emerging
questions about management of resources in the alignment of
abilities and needs. But this in itself constitutes, surely, no crippling objection to Marx, for it must be a commonplace of even
the most concrete of visions that their descriptions are replete
with the experiences of the relative failures of the present and

merely pointed with the fewer proleptic experiences of what the future could be coaxed to bring.

Marx's own life is a case in point, and it is not at all odd that this should be so, for it is usually the case with religions or their substitutes that the life of the founder contains in its own concrete form the essence of the religion. The life of Marx, on any objective account, shows not only that labour must not be taken to mean merely manual or physical labour, but also that he, like others, poured his life into his work for the benefit of humanity and not for any motive which a capitalist could ever recognize. Hence the story that Marx unfolds in his analysis of societies old and new, like the story of his life, details his vision of present and future with quite unequal clarity but with the same concrete intentionality. Before we finally try to decide how we are to take Marx's philosophical work, we might pause to notice the heart of his vision, the essence of Marxism.

## *Marx's 'relations of production': The source of social structures and ideologies*

One single phrase can take us to the heart of the matter: 'relations of production'. 'In the social production of their existence,' Marx wrote, 'men inevitably enter into definite relations of production which are independent of their will.'[12] That last phrase must surely be amongst those which have given some support to the view that Marxism, as dialectical materialism, revealed the laws of material nature by which the human race would be carried willy-nilly to its future state. The emergence of this view owes something no doubt to Engels, for it is Engels rather than Marx who on so many occasions suggests the reduction of what was thought to be mind or spirit to the physical laws of the material constituents of the world, and it was Engels who in his panegyric on Marx likened the latter's philosophy of human history to Darwin's theory of evolution.

This view is similar in one important respect to yet another and more recent interpretative tradition, for Marxism, like the religions for which it can be a substitute, has its officers interested in imposing orthodoxy and its rival parties each offering its original truth. The neo-structuralist interpretation of Louis Althusser, for example, also reduces the input of the human subject to disappearance point, though now the favourite supporting text from Marx is the sentence from the Sixth Thesis on Feuerbach which declares that the human essence is the ensemble of social relations. But this text, too, is taken to mean that progress is governed by fully scientific laws, in this case the laws of social relationships, and that the whole history of the world is in effect, as David McClellan once put it, a process without a subject. How interesting that a long philosophical tradition which began with complaints that a divine subject was crowding out a human subject should have ended in versions of Marxism which can tolerate no subject at all?

The debate about such views usually elicits quite contrary assessments of Marx's writings. Are the early writings in which Marx talks in the most humanistic terms to be regarded as infantile or at best ideological, and the later writings, *Capital* for example, as the scientific analysis of objective laws? Or are the later writings to be seen as the continuing quest for the concrete detail of human social behaviour which the humanist vision of Marx inevitably requires for its practical power? Into this large debate I do not have the competence to enter with any authority. My preference for the latter view of his writings and for the humanist thrust of his philosophy is based partly upon my own readings in Marx, but partly also, I have to confess, upon my conviction that this is the only reading of Marx which could sustain an ecumenical encounter with other humanist views, whether theistic or atheistic, in a world which is in ever greater need of such ecumenism.

So I take Marx to be a true follower of Feuerbach in this at least, that he did wish to make the human subject the real subject of human history. Because he wished to see this human subject more concretely than Feuerbach succeeded in seeing it, he insisted that it was to be defined not in terms of abstractly conceived attributes, however admirable these might be, but in terms of those relationships into which people inevitably enter in the course of the inevitable process of creating their lives and their world. I thus take the inevitability to refer to the process of creating and to the fact that it engenders our most basic social relationships, not to the precise form of relationships into which we may in the future enter. These precise forms we are now capable of designing as we create a better world, and they will always be in essence, in Marx's view, relations of production.

Of course, such freedom of input by the human subject is finite freedom. It is curtailed by the structures and contents of human beings and of things. Furthermore, in all ages past human beings were much more at the mercy of forces natural and social which they did not quite understand and could not control. And in all these ages religion, as opium, relieved the pain. More than this, it kept alive the hopes of a better world and, as 'the sigh of the oppressed creature', it gave voice to real human distress, and to human protest at all inhuman conditions. Only when these conditions are changed in practice and not, as Feuerbach seemed to think, when a theoretical critique of religion has been completed, will religion be no longer necessary; then it will simply wither away. The theoretical critique of religion is merely the prelude to the critique of concrete, inhuman conditions which religion simply reflects.

It is crucial to this version of the practicalist thesis to insist that it is in the relations of production, in those active relationships which are constituted in the very process of producing our lives, that success or failure, redemption or damnation, truth or untruth, subsists. Reality is essentially relational, as Hegel well knew, and the concrete truth must therefore consist in active relationships, the same kind of active relationships of production in which up to now the untruth of the human condition has been embodied and in which it has therefore been real. If we accept, then, as there is every reason to accept, the dehumanizing effects of the capitalist system—the manner in which and the extent to which people enslave themselves to their own products—and if we consider the prospect of liberation, however poorly we can at present predict the fine detail of a truly liberated humanity, the question to Marx is at last sufficiently pointed to provoke some sort of answer, the question, namely: how are we to see the role of Marx's own philosophical work in this liberating process? Was his philosophizing merely another theoretical interpretation of the world, or part of a praxis which in fact changed the world?

Needless to say the determinist interpretation of Marx would render that question itself otiose; indeed, if we are to be entirely logical here, it would render Marx's total philosophical output unnecessary, for irrefragable laws of history make even awareness of their existence altogether unnecessary. Hence, it must also be conceded that the very success with which Marx in his later writings revealed the iron logic of the self-destructive nature of capital itself militates against the usefulness to human agents of his having revealed it. Just as, in religion, if we are all already saved, there is little or no point in telling us about it. But if, as I have done, one rejects such a determinist reading of Marx, then it would seem that the role of Marx's writings was to evoke the correct kind of participatory experience, to call for and to accompany the recognition of slavery as slavery and, partly in this way, partly by going tentatively beyond this, to inspire the probing steps that could presage a future liberation. His writings, particularly in their more imaginative parts—and it takes a very great deal of imagination to be able simultaneously to see what is under one's nose and to see it transformed—provide the story which accompanies and interprets the action, and which together with the action constitutes the human drama.

There is good reason to believe that Marx in his own production obeyed the norms of the practicalist thesis which he himself so stoutly championed. He wanted by means of his concrete descriptions and critical analysis to make the consciousness of the oppressed fit the facts of their changing lives. Even philosophers like Kolakowski who do not believe in the continuance of something called Marxist doctrine as such, and who are totally disillusioned with those institutions which have attempted to rule large parts of the world in its name, are still happy to allow that Marx at one and the same time enabled us to understand how man is formed by the struggle in nature and society to humanize the world and how that struggle itself forms and is formed by human imagination, so that theory and practice are indeed inseparable. The practicalist thesis thus transforms the philosophy of imagination, and brings to light the clear structure of There-being's thrown-project.

## Marx's critique of religion

If one turns now to the classical Marxist critique of religion one need only notice that it is more concrete than Feuerbach's critique, just as Marx's concept of human nature is more concrete than Feuerbach's. Just as human nature is defined according to the ensemble of social relations, so religious creeds and institutions are mirror-images of human societies. The religious systems prevailing in pre-democratic societies reflected in their hierarchical structures and their heavenly visions the imperial, regal, or feudal structures of political society, and the sanctions of religious moralities were designed to remind each one of the duties of his or her state in life. Even in the new democracies of France and the United States, in which the separation of Church and State was loudly trumpeted, Marx pointed out that religion, like private property, was simply relegated to the private or civic sphere where the same old slavery, the same class distinction and discrimination continued, with the same old religious sanctions. God rewarded and the churches welcomed those who worked hard to accumulate wealth, and both sides agreed with equal enthusiasm that Marxists necessarily had to be atheists. There is no finer corroboration of Marx's views about religious petrifaction of the social status quo than the continuing willingness of Christian spokesmen to describe as Communist or Marxist, and therefore atheist, any who would in any way challenge the capitalist code.

And yet it is not altogether fair to Marx to complain, as Christians who want to have it both ways sometimes do, that he saw only establishment or Constantinian Christianity and that he ignored the prophetic, the critical, and the progressive elements which had always been an important part of the Judaeo-Christian tradition. For Marx did recognize the powerful expressions of human distress which are so prominent in a religious language and ritual that is deeply concerned with sin and its consequences. 'Religious distress', he wrote, 'is at the same time the expression of real distress and the protest against real distress. Religion is the sigh of the oppressed creature.' Only after these words did he write that religion is 'the opium of the people'.[13] Engels, too, in his historical analysis of the Peasant Wars in Germany at the time of the Protestant Reformation, contributed some concrete detail to the thesis that religion has exercised a critical function in society and has inspired people to back away from the bonds of their self-imposed slavery. But it is Ernst Bloch, in his powerful work *The Principle of Hope*, who, still a Marxist though a non-conformist one, re-read the whole of the Judaeo-Christian tradition from the perspective of the prophetic, the messianic, the apocalyptic, while freely acknowledging that these all too frequently belonged to the heretical fringes and not to the central establishment.

So Bloch prefers Genesis 1: 27, together with Genesis 3: 5, where man is made in the image of God and desires to be like God, knowing good and evil, to Genesis 2: 7 where man is made from dust, to which it is his bleak destiny to return. He prefers Moses the rebel exodist and his God ('I will be what I will be') to the establishment God of kingly covenants and Temple priests; the prophets' visions, which often harkened back to the desert period, to the political manipulators, even the Maccabean revolutionaries, for revolutions too often turn the wheel full circle. He prefers Job to Job's comforters, Münzer, the leader of the Peasants Revolt, to Luther, and Schweitzer's Jesus of history to Paul's divine blood-sacrifice. For within all these preferred manifestations of Judaeo-Christian religion lie for Bloch the hidden prospects of the ultimate *Humanum*, the finally human. And that is still the point for a Marxist, that even in its most active protest against human distress religion is still but the fantasy reflection of humanity's own highest qualities, in this case the quality of infinite hope, always revolutionary and creative of new forms of human life in this world.

We have not yet reached the point, then, at which Christianity can protect itself against Marxist reductionism—for it cannot do so by complaining that Marxist critique is confined to establishment Christianity—and Marxism is by far the most powerful form of reductionism which Christianity has had to face recently; psychological and sociological forms are pale copies by comparison, the same logic transmuted to a different and minor disciplinary mode. Much less have we reached the point at which Christianity can open up for Marxism the possibilities of a genuine dialogue in which Marxism could discover new ways of relating to religion and Christianity could discover new ways of being the praxis which in essence it always has been. Perhaps that point can only be reached by returning to the second question which we put to Marx, namely, could Marx's vision find a positive place, as Feuerbach's we suggested could not, for what Hegel once called 'the labour of the negative'?

## The meeting point of Marxism and Christianity

The prophetic, the messianic, the eschatological, the apocalyptic are first and foremost ways of dealing with the negative. The negative takes the form of deprivation and oppression and finally for human beings the form of death. The purpose of philosophy, Plato announced, is to train one to die. Heidegger's There-being is a being-unto-death, watching for being through the veil of nothingness, and trying through that deep contemplative action to live an authentic human life. Thus Western philosophy has always stressed that no philosophy worthy of the name can claim the slightest success until it has dealt with death. This is not because of any morose obsession with death as the ever-threatening end to the lives we know; nor could success be measured by the power to paint pictures of another life after the day on which clinical death occurs. On the contrary, death as the human form of the threat of nothingness is a dimension of the experience of everyday life for self-conscious beings. Philip Larkin, in his poem 'Aubade', wrote powerfully of 'what's really always there: unresting death':

> And so it stays just on the edge of vision,
> A small unfocussed blur, a standing chill,
> That slows each impulse down to indecision.
> Most things never happen: this one will
> And realisation of it rages out
> In furnace-fear . . .[14]

In such lines as these he evoked the constant power of death to drain the life from life, to weaken with apprehension the pulse of every nascent impulse, to mask pervasive fear with destructive rage.

So it is clear that death as the human form of the threat of nothingness, the definitive human form of the negative, enters into the fabric of every form of relationship, including relations of production. Much will depend, therefore, on how in practice we deal with the daily threat of nothingness. Much of the malformation or transformation of all our relationships must depend on this, and this is all the more true of relations of production in that, as Marx so rightly perceived, they are themselves formative of all the other natural and social relations into which we enter and from which we weave the very fabric of the human condition.

Marx began with relations of production. Different relations of production, he said, were appropriate to different stages in the development of the material forces of production. When land was the main material force of production feudal relations prevailed; when capital took over, relations of production change and with them all other relationships between and amongst the rulers of the world and the ruled. But have Marx and his followers gone deeply enough into these foundational relations? Are there already options within the ways in which I relate both to the material forces and to my fellow human beings which are even more basic than the operative ways in which I use the former to co-create better lives with the latter? Can you see from my behaviour at any and every stage of economic development, how I view all the material things which are under the universal sign of finiteness, and all the people who bear with me the common mark of mortality? Can I relate to real beings and things only with fear in the face of their constant advertisement of our common fragility, or with joy at their continued giving? The answer to that last question has at least as much practical import as the answer to any of the other questions which Marx subsequently asks about relations of production, for fear and joy are respectively the most destructive and the most constructive of human emotions. The question about our ability to deal in praxis with finiteness and mortality is therefore as crucial for a Marxist as for any other philosopher or theologian, and it has to be answered now.

It is commonly conceded that Marx did not see this question too clearly. Consequently, he did not do much to answer it. But Bloch saw it, and answered it. Death, being a dimension of daily experience, wears the familiar faces of familiar things. At the present time, for millions who die of starvation in a world of plenty, death wears the face of capitalist European Common Market economics, for example, which stockpile food and drink in massive 'mountains' and 'lakes'. But Bloch knows very well that even if we were to reach the Marxist future in which all economic-political problems were solved, death would still face us. In fact, death and the 'heralds of nothingness', as Bloch calls them, would simply wear new features, as yet largely inconceivable. And how should we then cope with death, and in coping with death cope with nature and with others?

Bloch's answers are surprisingly traditional, for all the individuality of his particular power with words. He writes about the veiled 'I', the mysterious ego which is so immersed in and which yet transcends all the experiences which make up its life story, so that, surviving each experience to go on to others, it begins to seem indestructible. He writes about the purely empirical evidence of dying, such that the theory of death as annihilation is no more surely founded than the theory of immortality. Indeed, he sometimes writes about life—'a young life, a life from the beginning, newly granted, unlocked, and poured out to us, over and over again'[15]—in language almost reminiscent of Hegel's spirit moving in our spirits through the world, never-ending. And at times he even envisages an almost ecclesial dimension of the future classless society which must be open to such depths or heights of human vision, 'a necessarily and a priori socialist-oriented church facing new contents of revelation'.[16]

One is not, of course, entirely dependent upon Bloch to show us that there are contact-points with Marxism which make a genuine dialogue between Marxism and religion possible. For Marxism, like any other philosophy, must sooner or later deal with death just as any religion which claims to be more than a form of escape clause in the human contract with the rest of finite reality must take fully into account the kind of concrete description of the human condition in this world, and the primacy of praxis, which Marx's vision continues to provide. Now no religion takes death as seriously as does Christianity. No other religion sets at the very centre of its creed and its cult the actual

worship of a *crucified* man. Christianity takes the willingness to
be crucified as the highest ethical model of its moral code, and
crowns each of its four major Scriptures with the unrelieved
detail of this ancient death. If any religion can meet Marxism at
the point at which Marxism most needs supplement, surely Christianity, if it can overcome its acquired and excessive other-
worldliness, can do it.

It must be said that Bloch is the best that the Marxist tradition
can offer in answer to the problem of dealing with death in life,
and that it is not good enough. Bloch did not write enough on
death to support any rigorous assessment, but what there is suggests too much of the veiled and spiritual self passing through the
successive experiences of life and, in the kind of Platonic option
least attractive to the practicalist thesis, somehow surviving it all.
Here are hints of the kind of Platonism which, full-blown, gives
rise to distinctions between soul and body and which, by
reserving real salvation for the former, fails to deal with movement and change in this world, with separation and pain, with
failure, in short, in all the concreteness of its material, historical
forms.

In order to appreciate how Christianity deals with the vagaries
of material history it is not necessary to adopt an exclusivist
Barthian view of Christianity, and it is not wise to concentrate
too much upon the actual execution of Jesus. For however much
Christians may stress the uniqueness and ultimacy of Jesus, it is
at the risk of diminishing God that they deny that whatever he
brought into history was there in some initial form before him;
that the Word by which the world was fashioned and which took
human form as Jesus of Nazareth (and *thus* became ultimate for
humans?) was also the light which enlightens every man who
comes into the world; that the practical options which Christians
now place before people were always in some incipient and original way ready to reveal themselves in nature and history, and in
all the philosophies, religious or otherwise, which nature and
history have suggested to man's enquiring mind.

Exclusive concentration upon the more immediate circumstances of the death of Jesus can actually obscure much that it has
to reveal about the Christian form of training to die. The

obscurantism often takes the form of confining the redemption of the race to the event of the cross; more infrequently it takes the form of a romance of death and suffering which is the polar opposite of the true Christian way through these inevitable things. In no philosophy of life worthy of the name is the training to die exclusively focused upon the performance or endurance of a particular final event at some uncertain future date, like training for the Cup Final. It must be, rather, a training to deal daily with things and people and with the heralds of nothingness which are always present in all of these in the concrete forms of finiteness and fear. The lesson of the death of Jesus can thus be learned only by those who can truly see it as the consummation of his life; and the essence of Christianity is to be found in those relations to persons and things which lie deeper within the relations of production and which, once we are made to feel their intrinsic power and to undergo their formative influence, initiate us into the joy of true love and direct for the best the whole process of creation. The story of dying during life in order to live, of losing one's self in love and thereby saving it, and of the encounter with the power to do all this, must yet be told. So, if this chapter ends with some thoughts about our knowledge of the actual death of Jesus, it is only for the purpose of illustrating by reference to the consummate event some points about praxis. It is in order to relate Christianity to Marxism at that point at which Marx seems open to completion, and in such a way as to emphasize a common allegiance to the practicalist thesis. But only when one knows where to encounter the power, and how to assimilate the life of Jesus, can one fully understand his consummate death. And that must come later.

## Our knowledge of Jesus' death

When I wrote *Jesus the Man and the Myth* I still felt that majority opinion in New Testament scholarship was telling me that substantial details about the arrest, the trial(s), and the execution of Jesus were available through the appliance of historico-critical methods to the New Testament text; and so I felt that the death of Jesus, in addition to being central to Christian faith, provided the best entrée to the quest for the historical Jesus. I believe as strongly as ever that Jesus, in the characteristic features of his career, is fully accessible to us, but the kind of consideration which has filled this and the first chapter has changed my mind about the manner in which Jesus is so accessible.

Redaction criticism was the form of New Testament criticism most in vogue when I was researching and writing *Jesus the Man and the Myth*, and its forte was to be able to distinguish the contribution of the evangelists themselves from the traditional material which they inherited and used in the final construction of their gospels. The supposition remained ambient that some of the traditional material might then be traced back to Jesus' lifetime or, at the very least, that some of it might be shown to contain specifically historical reminiscences of the life of Jesus.

The intervening years have been few, yet a number of factors have combined to alter that general perspective, particularly on the passion narratives in the four gospels. The simple factor of increased practice of redaction criticism of the passion narratives has rendered increasingly obvious the fact that it is exceedingly difficult to determine which parts of Mark's account are made up of traditional material. Although this is naturally easier with the other evangelists, at least two of whom used Mark, it is not easy with these either. In fact the more Mark was studied the more attention was drawn to his own literary creativity throughout the passion narrative, as indeed throughout the gospel of which that narrative is so integral a part, though he did undoubtedly use some traditional material. And the more Matthew and Luke were studied the more obvious became their indebtedness to Mark's literary creation. In addition, where traditional material is identified with some confidence—and it can confidently be said that Mark inherited a tradition of presenting Jesus as the suffering just man whom God would vindicate—this need be no more a matter of specifically historical reminiscence than Mark's own literary composition.

Behind Mark's story of the arrest, trial, and execution of Jesus, then, no more of specifically historical reminiscence may now be detectable than would assure us that Jesus was in fact executed as a result of a sentence passed by Pilate, though he was *perhaps* led before some Jewish authority also on that occasion. It seems more and more likely that the device of a trial within which the substance of the account of Jesus' last hours is set is to be attributed to the literary creativity of Mark's story rather than to any detailed memories. And why does Mark tell of Jesus' sentencing in this form? John R. Donahue suggests: 'Mark composes a trial of Jesus precisely as trial to meet the experiences and demands of the community for which he is writing, a community caught up in civil strife and trials in the years during and immediately following the Jewish war.'[17] In short, the followers of Jesus were in the years around AD 70 truly 'on trial' for their lives before Jews and Romans alike. The new 'way' was facing for many of them the ultimate test. So Mark has Jesus' status as God's true Messiah—a closely kept secret up to this point—revealed now, indeed proclaimed, at the very climax of his trial; and he follows this up with an execution narrative which has Jesus' title nailed to his cross, the confession of divine sonship addressed to a crucified man. Hence the one whom his readers profess to follow is one whose fidelity in ultimate trial makes him God's anointed; his exaltation to divine sonship—that is to say, his resurrection—takes place on a Roman cross; and he who suffers and dies like this will rule the future kingdom of God as the apocalyptic figure of the Son of Man. That is Mark's message in the passion narrative, and indeed in all his gospel, to those who would follow Jesus.

Mark's narrative of the trial and death of Jesus is therefore his own literary creation to an extent hitherto unrecognized. Mark's trial and execution is a narrative apocalypse; so, indeed, is his whole gospel. And yet, it is maintained, recognition of all this makes Jesus more and not less accessible to those who at any time would dare to follow him. How can this be?

There are at least three concentric circles through which one can be successively drawn by the centripetal magnetism of the *point* of Jesus' death, a point from which one might then see the significance of his whole life. The outer circle consists of the literary creation which Mark has left us, and other literary creations, some of which, perhaps in the form of 'oral literature', preceded Mark—stories, for example, of the death of Jesus as acts of a martyr—others of which followed in close dependence upon Mark—the passion stories of Matthew and Luke, for example, and then the passion story of John's gospel, and the story of Stephen's martyrdom in Acts, and all the acts of Christian martyrs, early and late. One can agree that the truth of the death of Jesus is recoverable from Mark's story, indeed preserved superbly in Mark's story, only if one realizes how much of a story there is of necessity in all that passes for history. Or, if one insists on operating at the outset with a clear-cut distinction between history and story, one simply has to realize sooner or later how much of the truth about historical people and events requires the imagination of the story-teller, the creativity of the literary artist, for its telling. Those who still remain unconvinced of this might look at Mary Warnock's piece on 'Religious Imagination' in the book of that title.

Mention of all the other acts of martyrs, before and after Mark's passion narrative, can draw one through to the next circle, and bring one again to the point of praxis. For many men and women did die like Jesus in consummate witness to his life, and they still do. Their deaths through the ages, together with the ever-present threat of death to other Christians at other times and places, represent in the form of this consummate witness a most practical access to the historic Jesus. Such acts of *historical imagination in practice* are surely amongst the most powerful ways in which an incarnate spirit that conquered death in death, and therefore in all of life, can still be accessible in any age. But the literary and the practical forms of access to Jesus are not in competition; indeed, as Mark's paradigmatic passion narrative proves, they are not altogether separable. Mark cast his narrative in the form of a trial because in praxis his fellows were on trial for their lives; fidelity in praxis and fidelity in the story were therefore mutually supportive and mutually dependent. Mark's story could sustain a wavering one when the following of Jesus became unusually dangerous and the temptation emerged once again to redefine Jesus' divine sonship in more escapist terms; but Mark's story could hardly have been told if no great fidelity had proved itself in practice during the years that separated Mark from a lonely death at the Place of Skulls.

The third and inner circle through which one may be drawn to the point of the death of Jesus becomes obvious to those who notice that within all four passion narratives in the gospels there is a graphic description of a ritual meal. This meal has been known from earliest times as the *anamnesis*, the re-presentation of the death of Jesus, and it is the single ritual distinctive of Christians which certainly came to them from the founder. It is the inner circle for a variety of reasons. It unites story and action; it is a dramatic or symbolic act in which people can participate at any time, whether particular persecution is present or not; and because it is a symbolic action, bearing the same relationship to daily action as poetic metaphor does to daily speech (that is, revealing the deepest and richest possibilities imaginable in daily life), it is closest to the point of the death of Jesus in pointing the way in which the fear of death is conquered in all of life. This ritual taking with thanks the staff and symbol of life, this breaking of bread and pouring of red wine, is praxis in its most inspiring and powerful form since it is symbolic praxis or drama. It is creative imagination in action.

There remain, therefore, these three forms of the act of historical imagination: the biblical narrative, the deaths of martyrs, and the ritual drama. And the greatest of these, for the reasons just given, is the ritual drama, the Eucharist. As words from the pen of the creative writer can evoke the heights and the depths, and inspire the human effort to probe them, so the ritual drama, the most comprehensive of art forms, can call up a spirit and infuse a power into ordinary life. If divine spirit exists in Jesus it is likely to be encountered in Eucharist, just as imagination, now also a form of praxis, gives access to the historical Jesus, the faith by which he lived and died, the spirit that was incarnate in his life, death and destiny.

But it remains for further chapters to say if and how the divine can be encountered through the Eucharistic *anamnesis* of the death of Jesus; how this death was truly the consummation of a life in which fear was already conquered and replaced by joy and hope; and how eucharistic praxis can inspire all praxis. The simple task of this chapter was to point to the revolution in modern civilization which gave rise to the practicalist thesis, to show Marx as the one whose creative imagination gave to the world the most impressive form of alternative praxis since the era of world religions began, and to suggest the point at which Christian and Marxist imaginative praxis are still open to each other.

# 3

# The Way (ii): The Truth that is done

Most theologians have felt at some time or other the abstract nature of theology. Or, if they have not felt it, they have no doubt been reminded of it by those who put themselves forward with a kind of inverted pomp as just ordinary people. In fact theologians are often grieved to discover that people whose professions would seem to make them natural allies often join in this critical chorus. Pastors and schoolteachers can be heard to claim a kind of pastoral involvement with what they choose to call the real world, and 'abstract' is by no means their most damning adjective for theology. 'Esoteric', 'unintelligible', and 'irrelevant' are even more dismissive alternatives.

Theologians who by and large are born, live, and die, mule and puke (in Shakespeare's elegant phrase) like anybody else might be pardoned for wondering what world they are thought to be involved with other than the allegedly 'real' one of which their critics speak. They may protest that theology, like any other discipline, must evolve a technical language of its own if it is to make any clear and distinct progress, a language which will serve as international currency, a kind of disciplinary esperanto. In more belligerent moments—and theology from the beginning has been eminently notable for the belligerence of its practitioners—theologians may retort that the more pastoral types amongst their critics are themselves purveyors of poor theology, the product either of obsolete forms of theologizing from the recent past or of extremely amateurish efforts in the present. Their critics, they may say, are facsimiles of themselves in childhood or senility.

Meanwhile, the real world seems to be going its own destructive way and paying a scrupulously balanced degree of near-total inattention to both sides in this internecine quarrel.

Faced with division and ambiguity within, indifference and ambiguity outside, the Christian can only look to his or her own party in the universal Christian movement and see what can be better done with it, looking to the other parties only for inspiration and not for a reason to criticize. So I shall look to the abstraction of theology, and I shall take the example of a doctrine—since all doctrine is distilled theology—which is arguably the very centre of Christian doctrine, the doctrine expressed most abstractly as that of the divinity of Jesus. I want to see if this doctrine is really concrete and relevant—just what so many formulations of this doctrine, both traditional and modern, are widely thought not to be.

## The Divinity of Jesus

The origin and development of the Christian conviction about the divinity of Jesus is mostly assumed to have been a predominantly verbal affair. That is to say, claims to the effect that Jesus is divine were verbally expressed either by Jesus himself or on his behalf by biblical authors. These claims are in turn supported either by miracles (above all, the resurrection), which for the vast majority of believers really refer to further claims that such events did in fact occur, or by further claims concerning the divinely inspired status of Scripture and its consequent inerrancy. Finally, these 'raw' claims concerning the divinity of Jesus are developed through great masses of abstract reasoning, both ancient and modern, mainly attempting to show how Jesus' divinity can be harmonized both with the divinity of the God he called Father, and with his full and true experience of the human condition. This development was in turn distilled into such traditional doctrinal formulae as that which claimed that the 'Word' of God made flesh in Jesus was *homoousios*, 'one in being or substance' with the Father, and another which claimed a 'hypostatic union' in Jesus of a divine nature and a human nature.

Now it is, of course, quite unnecessary to question the validity of any of this. Some claims must have been made by Jesus, however implicitly. Some unusual events must have accompanied his mission and that of his followers. Questions about the very nature of divinity certainly arose. And theology has no real need to apologize for the technical language which it has evolved over time.

What may, however, be doubted is this: that this abstract, rational argument in favour of the divinity of Jesus and this unpacking of its meaning—this process so beloved of theology because of its propositional nature—could *account for* anyone's conviction that Jesus was divine.

Since divinity is in question it will not be surprising that there is a parallel here with belief in God in general. Theoretical arguments for God's existence have probably never generated such belief in anyone, any more than reasoned rejections of the God hypothesis have ever truly deterred it. Words have power admittedly, but this is primarily the power to evoke what is there and what, as a result of what is there and of our relating to it, might yet be. Language in essence is incantation. Human existence in its origin, continuation, and ending is largely at the mercy of powers which it does not control. Human beings have endeavoured from the beginning to name these powers, if only so as to distinguish the benevolent from the malevolent, and ultimately to recognize the ultimate power of life and death, the conventional name for which is the word 'God' and its various equivalents. Belief in God, in any of its amazingly varied forms, and even belief that God does not exist, in its various forms, is a function of human encounter with, and recognition of, the powers that surround us in the only world we know. It is not the result of verbal claims.

Verbal claims are demonstrative in the literal sense of that word: they are designed to point to the place or time or circumstance in which that power can be encountered which I believe to be the real and effective presence, the immanence, of God. The origin of belief in God is to this extent experiential, or better existential, rather than propositional. In the same way convictions about the divinity of Jesus originate in and are supported by a release of power, a kind of power somehow identified with his person. And such convictions, because of their connection with power rather than propositions, are not expressed primarily in propositions, though they may of course be so expressed, but in the transformation wrought by that same power in the lives of those who have encountered it. The *verification* of these convictions is in turn not a matter of propositional proof but a matter of the progress of that power coursing through the world in the lives, deaths, and destinies of those who have truly encountered it. The real presence of power in the world, its encounter and recognition—such are the key categories of religious conviction or religious faith, and it is no accident that they immediately remind us of categories which are characteristic of the language of both Eucharist and resurrection: real presence, encounter, recognition.

## The resurrection of Jesus

Roman Catholics often congratulate F. X. Durwell, in his recent book on *The Resurrection* (1960), for salvaging the resurrection theme from the peripheries of theology, where it acted only as a proof-miracle for claims about the divinity of Jesus or as a kind of proof and preview of the general resurrection, and for moving it closer to the centre of Christian theology. But a less biased historian would have to confess that this had already been done 200 years earlier by Reimarus, who is considered by many to be one of the most destructive critics of the Christian sources. What Reimarus noticed was that the resurrection material in the New Testament, far from confining itself to the revival of a corpse as a miraculous proof of some claim or other, or providing an anticipatory exemplar of something yet to come, is in fact already preaching in its own concrete imagery what later came to be known more abstractly as the divinity of Jesus, and that *that* preaching reveals its principal intent.

So it is that those we regard as our enemies are frequently more perceptive about us than those we believe to be our friends. For this observation by Reimarus was unquestionably correct: as a sermon attributed to Peter early in the Acts of the Apostles puts it, 'God has made him both Lord and Christ, this Jesus whom you crucified' (Acts 2: 36). An early letter, that of Paul to the Romans, said of Jesus the Christ that he was 'designated Son of God in power by the Holy Spirit *ex anastaseōs nekrōn* (at or from his resurrection from the dead), Jesus Christ our Lord' (Rom. 1: 4). Probably the earliest Christian creed, which contains all of the subsequent doctrine of Jesus' divinity in a nutshell, is 'Jesus is

Lord'. The intimations of divine status which emanate from that title are, though often elusive in content, well known; and there is more than ample evidence that from the beginning the centre-point of the resurrection preaching was the lordship of Jesus.

The most recent theology concerning the resurrection material in the New Testament raises two kinds of problem, and both kinds I would want for the moment to avoid. They have exercised a premature monopoly on the attention we devote to the resurrection material. By doing so they have prevented us from seeing the main thrust of the biblical material, and they have thus, incidentally, missed their own best chances of a satisfactory solution. I believe this is because they are, each in its own way, hangovers from a primarily proof-miracle approach to the resurrection of Jesus. First, there is the problem of deciding whether the appearances of the Risen/Lord were bodily, physical, in epistemological terms truly empirical-sensual, or whether they were on the contrary spiritual-visionary. The second problem is deciding whether the kind of scriptural material I have just quoted is to be taken to mean that Jesus was shown to his disciples to be Lord at the resurrection, or whether these texts suggest that he actually became Lord through the resurrection. I call these problems hangovers from the proof-miracle view of the resurrection (and one must remember that the proof-miracle view is itself part and parcel of a propositional model of the origin and development of the belief in the divinity of Jesus) because an event must be publicly observable if it is to be classified as a miracle, and that is normally taken to imply in the case of the Risen/Lord a body in principle recognizable as his by anybody who had ever met him.

As far as the first problem is concerned, it is quite instructive to note that so many who seem to wish to get away from the proof-miracle reading of New Testament resurrection material seem, nevertheless, trapped by its characteristic concerns. In their historico-critical investigation of the origin of this material, they lead us back to what they call faith-experiences as the remote source of extant stories, in order to deter us once and for all from looking for proofs of the faith of our forefathers in the faith. Yet these theologians continue to talk of the resurrection of Jesus as the source of faith for his disciples, when the little faith they had

had was allegedly destroyed by his death. But they do not give us any explanation of what it was about the encounters with Jesus after his death that enabled them to have an effect which they apparently failed to have during his life. In the end, failure to deal with this question simply lends renewed credibility to the very proof-miracle approach which these theologians wish to set aside.

Take, for example, three recent Roman Catholic christologies, ranging from the more conservative to the more radical. It seems to me that in varying degrees the christologies of Kasper (*Jesus the Christ*), Küng (*On Being a Christian*), and even Schillebeeckx (*Jesus*) are inconsistent at worst, confusing at best, on the resurrection of Jesus of Nazareth. All want to give the resurrection of Jesus some role in getting the Christian movement going (again?) after the death of Jesus. According to Kasper, though Jesus saw his death as redemptive, and it could consequently be so understood by others, his cause was so bound to his person that his death could just as well have been considered the failure of his mission. So the historically evident dynamism of the new movement had to have what he calls an 'initial ignition' after Jesus' death, and this was the resurrection of Jesus. Yet he insists that 'Easter itself is an object of faith' (p. 131), and he describes the appearances of the risen Jesus as states of being possessed by Jesus (rather than objectively tangible events), as awakenings of faith, experiences of faith, encounters with Christ present in spirit. In answer to the question as to whether we are or are not talking of the resurrection of the person Jesus, he says: 'It is therefore not a separate event after the life and suffering of Jesus, but what is happening at the most profound level in the death of Christ' (p. 150).

Küng goes through much the same motions. 'Even the non-Christian historian' he writes, 'will not now dispute the fact that it was only after Jesus' death that the movement invoking his name really started' (pp. 343–4). Here again is the insistence that his cause was identified with his person, so that his death could only make it seem a failure (pp. 340 ff.). Once again we are told: 'Jesus' cause—which his disciples had given up as lost—was decided at Easter by God himself' (p. 352). And once again, just as we wait for some evidence of this act of God that was to get the movement now known as the Christian faith going again after its apparent failure, we are informed that 'the resurrection is not a miracle authenticating faith; it is itself the object of faith' (p. 360).

Schillebeeckx offers us a much more elaborate exegesis of the New Testament resurrection texts in the context of alternative early credal formulae about the present and future status of Jesus, but he still sets it all in the kind of scheme with which we are now familiar:

The death of Jesus put an end to the common life in fellowship shared by the earthly Jesus with his disciples—an end reinforced by their leaving him in the lurch. What was it then that after a time gave these same disciples reason to assert that they were once more drawn into a living, present fellowship with Jesus . . . what took place between Jesus' death and the proclamation by the Church? [p. 331]

The answer Schillebeeckx offers to this question centres on the conversion experiences of particular disciples, and first of all of Peter. Because they are already overlaid by more recently constructed resurrection kerygma in general and appearance stories in particular, these are now available to us only through the rather tortuous reconstructions of a scholar like Schillebeeckx. 'The appearances stories in the gospels', he writes, 'are no longer telling us about the initial conversion to Jesus' (p. 385).

In spite of great differences in detail, then, the same treatment of the resurrection is found in all three christologies. The origin of the Christian movement is attributed to something which occurred after Jesus' death, but when we enquire more closely after this something it turns out that no details of it can be given other than those which describe exactly the thing we wanted to explain, for all we can apparently be told is that the resurrection was the first irreversible faith-experience of the disciples. And since no further details of this faith-experience can be found we have no real reason for locating it after the death of Jesus rather than during his life or even at his death.

As far as the second problem is concerned, it is highly signifi-cant that those who feel themselves constrained to read in the texts quoted above the raising of Jesus *to* lordship feel that they must ask us to accept that the status newly conferred on Jesus after his death was nevertheless 'retroactively' and so *really* his long before that. Now real historical retroactivity in this sense is quite unintelligible to us. It is a piece of plain nonsense which only a Christian theologian who had become dreadfully entangled in his own theological underwear could be expected to invent. And so we find ourselves driven back to reading these texts as proclaiming that Jesus' lordship was revealed at the resurrection, a reading which is of course more congenial to the proof-miracle view. For we then have to ask once again what it was about Jesus' 'post-resurrection' appearances which made conviction about his divine status possible where his 'pre-resurrection' appearance in the flesh had failed. In the absence of an answer to this question, it is no wonder that the simplest terms of the proof-miracle approach once more recommend themselves. He claimed to be divine and he rose from the dead to prove it. Chosen disciples saw him alive in the flesh after they knew him to be dead. Ergo. We are back once more to verbal argument.

This is what I meant when I singled out two problems as hangovers from the proof-miracle approach to the resurrection and hinted that the accompanying headache will not be relieved until these problems cease to monopolize our initial attention. But legitimate concerns, about bodiliness and about the true revelation in history of the lordship of Jesus, do lie behind these two problems. Will these legitimate concerns be dealt with, and will the problems themselves become less intractable, if we refuse to let them monopolize our attention and take a different tack? I believe so, but it remains to be seen.

## A new look at the resurrection texts

Take it, then, that the resurrection material in the New Testament is basically the earliest expression of what later came to be known much more abstractly as the doctrine of the divinity of Jesus. Keep firmly in mind that this resurrection material *is* the preaching, the telling in story, the teaching of the divinity of Jesus, *not* of something which goes to prove the divinity of Jesus. A new perspective usually allows one to see aspects of a thing which did not stand out before, just as a new scientific hypothesis can direct one to look for phenomena hitherto undiscovered. What can one look for, then, from this new perspective on the resurrection material?

One should recall, first, that the question of divinity in general, the God-question as philosophers call it, has never really been a theoretical question, soluble at least in principle by logical argument, as to whether something called God does or does not exist. Even those most confidently described as atheists often realize that this is not the real issue. The real issue is the discernment of spirits, the recognition of powers, and the different kinds of living or of dying (or both) that encounter with such powers quite palpably makes possible. All human faith is quintessentially praxis, and religious faith, whether it be the faith of a theist or an atheist, a polytheist or a monotheist, is simply the highest, or in any event the most comprehensive, form of human faith. We are saved by faith, and by faith alone, for there is nothing that human beings see or do which is altogether outside of faith; but we are also damned by it, for faith in its myriad forms is simply our total response to the powers present and effective in our world which we encounter and recognize, or encounter and fail to recognize.

If one looks at the resurrection material in the New Testament from this perspective, one sees the appearance narratives in a new light, because one is led to look for an effective power or presence of the one called Lord in our world and in our history, and this very way of seeing things should in turn make one look further for suggestively close connections between resurrection/appearances and Eucharistic meals.

First, then, resurrection and appearances, as they are called. It is, I believe, a final by-product of the proof-miracle approach to the resurrection that resurrection and appearances were distinguished as two quite different kinds of event: resurrection itself was said to be an act of God and as such quite undetectable by human powers of perception. It took place 'invisibly' just after Jesus' death, and the canonical Scriptures are praised for not attempting to describe it. The appearances of the Risen/Lord, on the other hand, are events of an unusual but still quite different nature; they give tangible evidence of invisible resurrection which in turn provides evidence of divine status. So the usual story goes, and it is generally agreed across the lines which otherwise divide physicalists from spiritualists, for the simple reason that both have already, as the basic proof-miracle approach suggests, distinguished the divinity of Jesus from its evidential supports.

Now it is of course a necessary caution to observe that God is still hidden even in those events in which God's effective presence is thought to be encountered and God in consequence recognized. But it is quite another matter to imagine God doing things other than those things done in this world in which God is thought to be encountered. The first expresses the risk of faith, the second takes a diabolical liberty. Apply all of this to the resurrection of Jesus and it becomes clear—both from the point of view of the question of divinity as an encounter with power rather than a theory of absolute beings, and from the point of view of confining oneself to events experienced rather than inventing additional events—that the appearances of Jesus in which he is encountered and (finally) recognized actually *constitute* what we call the resurrection of Jesus, in so far as this can be experienced, rather than simply supplying subsequent evidence for it. Hence they constitute human experience of the divinity of Jesus since, as we saw, to say Jesus is risen is in essence to say he is Lord—though, like saying he is Lord, it implies many more things about him.

Questions of course come crowding in at this point of the argument, all the more numerous and complex the more cogent the argument is thought to be. How do the varied New Testament references to appearances and stories of some of them meet this new perspective? What is it about any of them that supports a view of them as encounters with power that at once convinced those affected that God was truly active and releasing a transforming, benevolent spirit into the world? And if those appearances/encounters with divine power were in effect confined to a short span of time after the death of Jesus, are later followers of Jesus not once more dependent on verbal claims from the distant past and the various supports and developments of these which theology itself supplies? And, finally, is not resurrection-as-appearances still a posthumous event which reveals as much discontinuity with the human life and death of Jesus as is implied by the proof-miracle view of the resurrection in its many forms? There is no simple and conclusive answer to all these questions, but there is one aspect of the appearance stories which the new perspective brings into view and which can go a long way towards suggesting a set of satisfactory answers to them. I refer to the Eucharistic context which the New Testament so often, both in narrative and in oblique reference, suggests for so many of the appearances of the Risen/Lord.

The New Testament would not allow anyone to argue that all the appearances took place during the course of Eucharistic celebration. Apart from appearances to Mary Magdalene and Paul, from which a Eucharistic setting is clearly absent, appearances are mentioned, such as one to Peter, for which no setting at all is supplied. Nor could one wish it to be otherwise for, however central to Christian life and experience we may want to argue the Eucharist should be, we would certainly not want to conclude that all enabling encounters with the Lord Jesus must occur at the eucharistic table. Yet the New Testament can surely be thought to suggest that an enabling encounter with the Lord is *normally* available at the Eucharist, and this does accord with the centrality of the Eucharist in Christian life.

The story of the disciples at Emmaus is of course the paradigm here, with its climactic statement: 'when he was at table with them he took bread and blessed, and broke it, and gave it to them. And their eyes were opened and they recognized him' (Luke 24: 30–1); 'Then they told what had happened on the road, and how he was known to them in the breaking of bread' (Luke 24: 35). But one can argue quite convincingly that the Eucharistic meal is also the setting for appearances in stories such as that in John 21: 1–14, John 20: 19 ff., Luke 24: 36 ff. (Mark 16: 14); and perhaps even more significantly that such general references to the appearances of the Risen/Lord as those found in Acts 1: 4 and 10: 41 reveal a general assumption about the Eucharistic setting of appearances. If we were to agree, then, that the Eucharist is the normal setting for an encounter with the Risen/Lord, we might well ask, what more can be seen from this perspective? Something scarcely noticed about the Eucharist, perhaps?

## The Eucharist

The most notorious theological theory of the real presence of Jesus in the Eucharist, and the most controversial even within contemporary Roman Catholicism, is the theory of transubstantiation, the theory that the substance of bread and wine is really changed into the body and blood of Christ (inseparable, of course, the theory explains, from his 'soul and divinity'), while the accidental forms of colour, taste, and so on, remain. The moment at which this substantial exchange is thought to take place has long been determined to be the moment at which the so-called 'words of consecration' are uttered over bread and wine by a validly ordained minister—the words of consecration refering to words attributed to Jesus at the Last Supper: 'This is my body; this is my blood.' One is immediately struck by the similarity of this theory to the more physical interpretations of the resurrection appearances. And is it not quite striking also that those who challenge the 'substantiation' theories so often do so by opposing spiritual presence or reception to physical, the very language used in the resurrection controversy? It might therefore be wise once again to avoid initially the present inter-church and intra-church controversies about transubstantiation, consubstantiation, transignification, etc., and to seek, as with the resurrection, a different, in fact a more biblical approach.

Much modern theology of the Eucharist reminds us, first, that in medieval times metaphysical 'substance' language usurped the more ancient and more promisingly ambivalent anthropological 'body' language; and, second, that modern 'moment of consecration' disputes replace a more ancient theology of emerging presence which was at once more petitionary and more inclusive of the whole Eucharistic drama and of the role of all its participants. When Paul—and he is the only New Testament writer who definitely does this—describes Jesus as saying 'do this in remembrance of me' (the Greek word for remembrance is *anamnesis*), the directive does not apply merely to the repetition of so-called words of consecration. It covers, rather, the communal breaking of bread and pouring out of wine and all that this dramatic symbolism entails. And if early Eucharistic liturgies have an *epiclesis* or two (an *epiclesis* is an invocation of the Holy Spirit), that does not mean that only then is spirit invoked. As Paul said, the Lord is the spirit, Jesus is life-giving spirit. The whole action of the whole group with the bread and wine is thus a prayerful effort to make Jesus present as power or spirit (the terms are often equivalent) in the whole eating and drinking group, so that it, with its shared life-giving food, may be the body of Christ in the world. This whole dramatic and symbolic action is *anamnesis* and *epiclesis* simultaneously; that is to say, it is a kind of memorial act or, better, a representational act which is intended to bring about a presence of power, and its very nature prohibits the allocation of such success as might be achieved to any particular elements or words within the drama. If the power or spirit (of) Jesus is present in the meal, this table-fellowship will be the body of Jesus in the world. It is considerations such as this that can lead us back to a more biblical theology of the real presence of the body of Christ and which can discover, incidentally, the closest relationship between Eucharist and resurrection.

Begin with Paul's word, with Eucharist as *anamnesis*. The word is capable of many meanings, but one meaning is clearly indicated by the occurrence of another word in three of the accounts of the Last Supper, those by Paul, Mark, and Matthew —the word 'covenant' in the phrase 'blood of the covenant' or 'covenant in blood'. For one principal meaning of the word *anamnesis* was to recall to God a covenant with the people or to recall to the people the terms of a covenant with God. In Israel's history 'covenant' referred originally to those suzerainty covenants between great kings and lesser ones whereby property, protection from enemies, and other blessings accrued to the latter on their observance of the covenant stipulation. Theologized, the term referred to expectations of God's grace consequent upon the keeping of what Israel believed to be His laws.

But what were the stipulations of the 'new' covenant which, according to this very early eucharistic imagery, Jesus had entered into with the God of Israel? They can be gleaned from many Eucharistic passages in the New Testament, for they recur quite regularly: they are to take, to bless God for, and to break in order to give (or, if one is thinking of the drink rather than the food, to pour out in order to give). So the very first celebrants of the only religious ritual which Jesus himself engaged in with them are recalling to God that Jesus took bread and blessed God for it—for it was God who was blessed in ancient Jewish custom, not things: the blessing basically thanked God for the gracious gift indicated on the particular occasion of the blessing—and that he broke it to give it again.

In doing this, of course, they were not recalling to God just one particular meal, for instance the Last Supper. Or if they did recall any particular meal it was because of its highly symbolic nature, its sacramental nature as later theology would say. For bread is the staff and symbol of life, and it was Jesus' taking of life with thanksgiving as God's gift, and his proven willingness to give it again to the point of body broken and blood poured out, that the followers of Jesus recalled to God. And it is this that the highly condensed symbolism of the Last Supper conveys. Jesus' words —of the bread, 'this is my body given for you'; and of wine in a cup passed round to be drunk, 'this is my blood of the covenant' —give to the common symbolism of bread and wine taken, blessed for, broken and poured out and given, its ultimate significance as a commitment of life itself. And not only for Jesus who saw and fulfilled that significance, but for all who would share in the ritual either with him or in his name.

For the recalling of covenants and their stipulations could never be only a recalling to God's memory, as if God tended to be a little forgetful. The covenant imagery is man-made, and so it leads naturally to anthropomorphism; it can also lead to the belief that a timely reminder to God of what Jesus accomplished will gain us grace without more ado. The *anamnesis* of covenants involves recalling their stipulations to the human covenanters also, and requires a recommitment on their part to attempt to live up to these stipulations. In the case of the covenant struck in Jesus' life and death this means a life, and if necessary a death, like Jesus. Paul said: I live now, not I, but Christ lives in me. This life of taking, blessing for, breaking and giving is the life of Jesus, it is Jesus *redivivus*, living again in others. Or, in language once more characteristic of Paul, it is the spirit (of) Jesus which, because it is the same spirit enlivening 'head' and 'members', makes the followers of Jesus his body in the world.

However, as this very language suggests, it is not simply in our power to live that kind of life. This power made perfect in weakness, this spirit of self-giving, the spirit of Jesus, is not naturally ours, so that we could claim merit for its exercise. Eucharist is sacrament and sacrament is prayer. This does not mean that one might as well talk as act. Actions speak louder than words and, in addition, as the traditional definition of a sacrament implies, sacraments effect what they symbolize. So one does ritually exactly what one then petitions to be able to do in the whole of one's life—one takes as gift, in thanksgiving, to give again. In other words, the symbol participates in that which it symbolizes: Eucharist is ritual invocation of the power to meet the covenant stipulations in life and in death. It is ritual invocation, in the form of *anamnesis*, of the power, the spirit of Jesus. This invocation takes explicit form in *epiclesis*, invocation of the spirit to bring to life the body of Jesus in the world. But the form of words merely makes explicit what the dramatic action, the ritual performance of the covenant stipulations, already symbolizes. Eucharist is simultaneously *anamnesis* and *epiclesis*, and when it works or is answered, the community which celebrates it is the body of Christ.

It might be well to remark at this point that it makes little difference to this account whether or not the Last Supper was a Passover meal. I do not say this merely because there seems to be considerable uncertainty in the gospel references to the date of the meal and in other relevant respects. I say it rather because the insistence that the Last Supper was a Passover meal can serve to detract from its primary symbolism. Once its primary symbolism is understood there is no harm, and indeed there can be much gain, in superimposing Passover symbolism in order to express to those who are familiar with such symbolism the liberation from slavery which participation in the meal can bring. But the primary symbolism of the meal must first be firmly in place. And the best way to make sure of that is to look to other important passages in the New Testament where the Eucharist is the subject apart from the accounts of the Last Supper in Paul, Mark, Matthew, and Luke.

In this way one can learn what it is that is truly distinctive of this single sacrament instituted by Jesus himself, what it is that distinguishes the symbolism of this meal from that of the many symbolic meals celebrated by so many different religious groups, and what, in more concrete detail than large phrases like 'self-sacrificing love' can convey, taking in thankfulness and breaking to give can imply.

In John's Last Supper there are no words said over the bread and wine at all, but the one who is master performs for the others the menial task of the household slave; the two occasions on which Mark treats the Eucharist as a feeding miracle (Mark 6, 8), giving food to those who need it, have a point too obvious to labour; and the power of the meal to reconcile those whom social theory and practice keeps carefully apart is already expressed in the earliest and briefest references to Jesus' table-fellowship—again it is his enemies who see the point most clearly: 'why does he eat with tax collectors and sinners?' (Mark 2: 16). Such radical revision of the nature of leadership, such willingness to give to others the necessities of one's own life, such practical love of the enemies of society —such is the kind of thing that Jesus' breaking of bread both symbolized and began to effect. But, as Jesus' broken body and spilled blood prove, human society will not stand for this; the symbolism of breaking and pouring out then becomes fearful and final for all. Contrast with this the relatively harmless business of exchanging substances or the over-general symbolism of escape from slavery and one begins to see what was really distinctive about this one sacrament which Jesus left to his followers.

## Resurrection, Eucharist, and Divinity

Resurrection means lordship, and it is in the encounters with the risen one that this lordship is experienced. Hence the appearance stories *are* the New Testament representations of the resurrection/lordship of Jesus. The nature of the lordship and consequent discipleship is even indicated in appearances/encounter stories: a spirit of forgiveness, of reconciliation, is released. The setting of these appearances/encounters is normally a Eucharistic meal. The question which now emerges concerns the nature of the relationship between appearances/encounters of the Lord Jesus and the Eucharistic meal. Put at its bluntest: was the meal merely the setting for the appearances or was the meal itself the encounter? The shortest route to an answer to this question lies through a number of themes which occur in the earliest presentations of both Eucharistic meals and encounters with the Risen/Lord.

## The theme of immortality

Take, for example, the theme of immortality, or, better stated, of victory over death. The Risen/Lord is said to be the first-fruits, the first instalment, and so the earnest of our resurrection (1 Cor. 15: 20); in early Christian theology the Eucharist was called the 'medicine of immortality'. The language of this latter theology was often very physical indeed: Jesus, or God, becoming bread and wine and this food and drink then becoming so much part of our flesh and blood that in this case alone no excrement resulted. So we consume the food from heaven and, as the old Jewish myth of the manna insisted—which Jesus referred to in John's Eucharistic discourse (John 6)—those who eat heavenly food do not die, unless of course they abuse it (1 Cor. 11: 30).

Now here is a theme which could lead us to suspect that encounters with the Risen/Lord are in fact identical with the celebration of Eucharist; that the latter is not just the occasion on which, once upon a time, the former also occurred. For if that were so, then our hope of victory over death, if it were not reduced to a very poor statistical probability, would be based on verbal promise and the 'proof from appearances' that the one who made the promise to raise us was as powerful as he said. In short we should once again, as in the case of faith in God, be reduced to actual report and verbal argument for the source of one of the most important convictions which human beings can entertain. And so we are led to suspect that resurrection/appearances and Eucharistic meals are both said to be the source of our victory over death because they are very much the same thing;

appearances stories normally have meal settings because normally the Eucharistic meal *is* the encounter with the lordship of Jesus. Emmaus is the paradigm.

But we must now press on to another theme which in Scripture and early theology was used to present resurrection and Eucharist. For if we stayed with the theme of immortality we might fall victim to the all too common impression that Jesus' resurrection, and a similar victory over death for us, has to do with some afterlife, that it is as little a part of our living and dying on this earth as it was of his.

In addition, if we were to fail to develop further this theme of the food of immortality we might well fall foul of the scriptural complaint that it is the spirit that gives life, while the flesh profits nothing, and that our account is too fleshly. I say too fleshly rather than too physical for the scriptural contrast is not between the spiritual and the physical or bodily—in an incarnational religion the spirit can never be too physical—but between the spirit and the flesh. Flesh is an existential term, not a physiological term. In theological language it connotes anything, literally any thing, person or act, from which we expect that which only God can give. So if any human being—and this includes Jesus of Nazareth—ever thought that he had in his possession a formula for changing bread into God or could appoint a special class of people to do this, and could by thus eating this bread gain the victory over death, that human being would have to be accused of dealing in flesh, of committing the fatal fault which John's Eucharistic discourse was anxious to warn against.

## The theme of spirit

The theme which most closely relates Eucharist to resurrection/appearance, then, the theme which correctly presents the source of our hope of victory over death, is the very theme which Paul used to identify the body of Christ in the world; it is the theme of spirit.

In the Bible and in early theology spirit is most frequently a word for God. It connotes a power or force decisive enough to be considered divine, mysteriously beyond all that is constitutive of our empirical world and yet most intimately at work within it.

Spirit, like the cognate terms 'Word' and 'wisdom', is a term used to indicate how that power can be encountered which one believes to be the very effective if still hidden presence of God in the world. What later theology in its abstract fashion refers to as the divinity of Jesus is most frequently expressed in the New Testament in terms of spirit, and very infrequently in terms of Word. It is by the Holy Spirit that Jesus is Son of God 'in power' through resurrection, so that the risen Jesus is himself life-giving spirit (Rom. 1: 4; 1 Cor. 15: 45). Luke and John in particular, when telling their stories of the appearances, include reference to this spirit being breathed into or given to Jesus' disciples. So if the general contention is correct, that the accounts of the appearances are accounts of the resurrection of Jesus, there is ample scriptural evidence to show not only that resurrection does mean the exaltation of Jesus by 'spirit' (God) to the status of spirit (a divine lordship), but that his followers' conviction about all this was due to their encounters with the life-giving spirit in which he imparted the same spirit to them.

Now there is far too much coincidence between this account of resurrection in terms of spirit and the earliest accounts of Eucharist, also in terms of spirit, for us to conclude that stories of appearances/encounters in Eucharistic setting do no more than tell of the occasions on which appearances/encounters simply happened to occur. The disciples of Jesus frequently gathered to break bread, as he had done with them, and sometimes on some of these occasions, in addition as it were, they also encountered the life-giving spirit, the Risen/Lord, who imparted this spirit to them? Unlikely, to say the least.

The scriptural origins of an early theology of Eucharist in terms of spirit are most likely supplied by Paul and John. First there is Paul's promisingly ambivalent imagery of the body of Christ. Ambivalent because one is not quite sure in a Eucharistic passage such as 1 Cor. 11: 17–34 whether body always refers to Jesus' own body or to the body of his followers. Promising because this very ambivalence can open one to the impression that Jesus is only really present when his followers are being fashioned into a body by his spirit. Indeed it can be very instructive at this point to notice that in this letter of Paul's his statement on the Eucharist (1 Cor. 11), in which this body imagery occurs, and his statement on the resurrection (1 Cor. 15), in which he talks of the spiritual body and of Jesus as life-giving spirit, form a kind of enclosure for a long section of the letter which is totally taken up with the spirit and the gifts and workings of the spirit, the spirit which makes Jesus and his followers one body, though each have different parts and roles within it.

John's major account of the Eucharist (John 6) is placed in quite a different geographical setting from other gospel accounts of the Last Supper, yet it is undoubtedly an alternative account. The reference to the imminent Passover provides the familiar opening motif, and although what follows immediately is a feeding miracle like Mark's, the ritual acts of Eucharist are unmistakably described: taking, giving thanks, distributing. Here the partaking of the bread of life is most graphically, most physically equated with eating Christ's body and drinking his blood, but here, correspondingly, the judgement is peremptory: it is the spirit that gives life, the flesh is of no avail.

Here is ample scriptural basis for an early theology of Eucharist in terms of spirit, a theology which shaped the early Eucharistic prayers as much as it shaped the commentaries and the catechesis, a theology which centred on the invocation of the spirit to make Jesus bodily present in the action with the bread and wine by making the community into the body of Jesus the Christ. One brief example must suffice here: the early thirdcentury Eucharistic prayer of Addai and Mari contains no Last Supper words over bread and cup, yet Louis Bouyer comments on the *epiclesis* of that prayer:

If we may take it that in the very archaic prayer of Addai and Mari the words 'thy holy spirit' applied to the Son are to be understood as the virtual equivalent of 'thy presence' or 'the power whereby thy glorified body is present to us' in the fashion of Old and New Testament writers (where God's glory was a way, like his spirit, of speaking of his powerful presence), the whole construction and meaning of the petition become perfectly clear and straightforward.[1]

Jesus' real presence in the Eucharist is described in terms of the coming of spirit, the powerful presence of God. In other words, in the Eucharist people encounter the power which they identify as the spirit of Jesus, and the spirit that is God, and let it breathe into them in the most bodily way possible, by taking bread, blessing God for it, breaking it and giving it to be eaten, bread which is the staff and symbol of all life.

Of the Eucharist, then, can be said precisely what could be said of the resurrection/appearances, namely, that Jesus is encountered as a spirit or power, as a life-giving spirit. Since spirit is a word for God, it can be added that for the one who has this experience, God is in Jesus reconciling the world to himself, or God's reign, or his kingdom, or lordship is palpable in Jesus' distinctive spirit. These are amongst the most elementary formulations of what later became known as the divinity of Jesus. Certainly at this stage the similarites between Eucharist and resurrection/appearances are far too great for mere coincidence.

## Eucharist as an encounter with the Risen/Lord

Is it seriously suggested, then, that the resurrection, palpable in the appearances, *is* the divinity of Jesus experienced, and that Eucharist *is* resurrection/appearance and hence divinity of Jesus experienced? The simplest answer to this complex question is: yes. Two qualifications already mentioned do not really diminish the simple straightforward force of that answer.

The first is that the Risen/Lord may of course be encountered without the eucharistic celebration. Indeed if that were not the case the Eucharist could be considered to have failed. For unless the kind of praxis which it symbolically initiates is carried over into the whole of life the power encountered is being confined instead of released in the world, and that, as we must shortly see, bears an uncomfortable resemblance to a person being confined to his grave. But apart from the change which the Eucharist, if it is not seriously flawed, must bring about in living in general so that the same power and presence, the same spirit, may be more broadly encountered, there are other ways designated in Scripture by which the Risen/Lord may be recognized.

One is in fact the expounding of Scripture itself so that, as the prevailing imagery puts it, eyes may be opened and the true Lord seen. Luke refers to this in his Emmaus story, and although on this occasion it does not seem to have worked on its own, it had greater success in the hands of Philip when he met the Ethiopian eunuch on the road to Gaza (Acts 8: 26–39). Then there are other rituals, other sacraments. There is baptism, which if it was not actually enjoined by Jesus himself was certainly practised by his earliest followers. Converts in Jesus' name went down to the watery grave and emerged again to live his risen life, so that Paul could say, 'by one spirit we were all baptised into one body' (1 Cor. 12: 13)—exactly the same imagery of spirit and body that was used for the Eucharist. In succeeding centuries the Christian community added other sacraments—the final number, seven, undoubtedly owing more to the mythical status of the number seven than to anything instituted by Jesus.

But one does not need to take this matter further. The medieval monk, Thomas Aquinas, said that all the sacraments were ordered to the Eucharist as to their end or goal—which implies that the Eucharist is the consummate, indeed the comprehensive, sacrament. It does fully what all the others do partially; it reconciles the sinner as does penance; it brings the spirit as does confirmation; it makes the union of man and wife a sign of Christ's union with his church; it challenges sickness, the harbinger of death, in the very presence of death itself, as extreme unction is meant to do; and it is its nature as a community action, a community meal, that gives the appointment or ordination of one who is to preside at it whatever significance such presidency may legitimately be thought to have. It is therefore a step in the right theological direction when Roman Catholics now celebrate all sacraments within the Eucharist, as means of refracting in different colours for different occasions its single white light. Though the Eucharist, then, is not the only means of encounter with the Risen/Lord, it is, both by reason of the kind of sacrament it is and by reason of its origin at the centre of Jesus' own life and death, the central means by which the Risen/Lord may be encountered.

The second qualification takes the form of the contrast already mentioned between spirit and flesh, or, as Paul rephrases it for the expounding of Scripture, between spirit and letter (2 Cor. 3), the enlivening and the deadening. It is possible for human beings, as their long and dismal record proves, to turn that which can give them life into a weapon of mutual destruction. The Scriptures have long been plundered by warring Christian theologians for batteries of texts to use against entrenched positions, and the spirit, which as all sides loudly proclaim breathes in these Scriptures, has thus been made demonic. The same human tendency to possess and to control can make the Eucharist flesh also, and it is this which prevents a proper understanding of the embodying of divine spirit, and which gives the bodily itself a bad name.

There are instructive parallels at this point with some New Testament stories of the resurrection appearances, stories in which Jesus has his hands and side poked by the incredulous, his legs grabbed by the over-enthusiastic. There are clear warnings in these stories that the Risen/Lord cannot be controlled and possessed in this way. Yet there are whole Christian communities today who attempt a similar form of control and possession with respect to the eucharistic body of Christ. Only *their* theology of Eucharist, *their* formula, *their* ministry can make Jesus present in the Eucharist. So he is possessed and controlled by easily checked criteria, none of which have anything directly to do with the particular spirit of taking and breaking open which the sacrament as such embodies and which will inform any body that truly celebrates it. Eucharist too is thus made flesh by the demonic spirit which tries always to possess and to control. But if Eucharist is celebrated in the spirit in which it was instituted, a spirit which would serve rather than dominate, give rather than hoard, then it is indeed an encounter with the Risen/Lord, the life-giving spirit does indeed make an appearance. Jesus is then really present in power, which means that people today are not dependent upon ancient stories, however reliably reported, for their convictions about what they call his divinity.

Are we then to conclude that in those appearances of the risen Jesus which occurred in a eucharistic setting it was the breaking of bread which made Jesus present, and there was in addition no actual physical presence of the man with whom the disciples had walked the dust roads of Galilee? It would, I think, be as impossible as it would be unnecessary to rule out on historical grounds such a physical presence. But it is very necessary indeed to point out that it is not such physical contiguity that enables one to encounter the Christ, the Lord. It is not sufficient here simply to remind oneself that physical contiguity is the most insignificant form of presence. Many a failed marriage testifies to the fact that continuing physical proximity can serve merely as the most painful and constant reminder of separation, of absence and loss. All that is true and evident, but the point about the presence of Jesus the Lord is best made by comparing Eucharistic meals after his death with those at which he presided before his death. In the latter, though he was as physically present as it is possible to be, this did not of itself enable anyone to encounter and recognize the spirit that made him what he was, the God who acted in him. Some actually felt that they encountered in him the spirit of Beelzebub, the demonic spirit, not God, not the holy spirit. Many more left him, some betrayed him, all misunderstood him to a greater or lesser extent for the greater part of their time with him. There is no short cut to the encounter and recognition of holy spirit. It is not available through simple profession of faith, however orthodox, through loud and frequent proclamation that Jesus is Lord (Lord! Lord!). Peter got the formula right in his famous confession to Jesus' own face, but in the process he missed the spirit of Jesus completely.

Encounter and recognition of holy spirit is thus not given through physical contiguity with Jesus either before or after his death. The mere physical presence of Jesus alive again after his death implied no more than it implied in the case of Lazarus; in both cases of itself it implied only that they were there again (You're back again! exclaimed their friends and acquaintances) and if it implied nothing further it implied that they would have to die once more. That is why Par Lindquist, in his marvellous novel on Lazarus, depicts the raised Lazarus as the deadest man who ever lived. In the taking of bread as gift and the consequent blessing of God for it and the breaking of it to give again in an overflow of the same generosity one has experienced, in this the lordship of Jesus is encountered and recognized, and this is no more difficult for us than it was for the earliest of Jesus' followers. Nor is it any easier—although as John may be taken to hint, we don't have his physical body around to tempt us to sit it on one of our many thrones. And we are dependent on those earliest followers only in the same way as others will be dependent on us, to continue to show how the life-giving spirit into which God (we therefore believe) made Jesus can be encountered and recognized.

So Jesus was Lord and life-giving spirit before his death, then, and it was as possible to encounter him as such, as possible to believe in him, before his death as it was after it? Of course; just as it remains as possible to miss his spirit after his death as it was before it. But if the main point of claiming that he was raised is to say that he is Lord, then was he not raised before he died? It is most emphatically necessary to answer that question also in the affirmative. For here lies the grain of truth in that otherwise nonsensical theory of the raising of Jesus to a status after his death which was nevertheless retroactively his during his life. However, if the grain is to bear fruit it must be properly cultivated.

## Jesus' victory over death

The phrase 'on the third day' is not meant to convey information about exact timing of an event; it is meant to convey, rather, the belief that God's consummate intervention is taking place. 'The son of man will be delivered up, and they will kill him, and after three days he will rise': this is not a statement about calendar dates; it is making a contrast between what men do and what God does. 'God has made Lord and Christ this Jesus whom you crucified.' It was in his life, and consummately in his death, in the ultimate breaking and pouring out, that Jesus became life-giving spirit. *In* life and above all *in* death he recorded the victory over death. John saw that most clearly of all the gospel writers, and that is why John has Jesus raised on Calvary, and has him breathe the spirit from the cross. It is in living the life of a man and in dying the death of a man that Jesus is life-giving spirit; to diminish in any way the force of this insight is to misunderstand to that extent the peculiarly Christian doctrine of incarnation, the doctrine that divine spirit became fully human.

Nothingness is the veil of being, as Heidegger said, and for human beings nothingness makes its presence felt most distinctively, most concretely, in the experience of death—an experience that we have in the course of life rather than at the moment of death itself when we are possibly not aware of anything very much. And only through that veil can being be reached; the dark passage is unavoidable. Further, there is no assurance within our possession that when we do finally go through the veil anything at all will be reached. Empirical evidence tells us that we disintegrate and go back to the earth to become once more part of the life-perpetuating cycle; so in old Irish religion the divinity (female naturally) was the land, and one of her commonest names was Brigid. We cannot say for sure that anything further awaits us. Hence the story of Jesus is profoundly tragic, and those who say that Christianity lacks the essential element of tragedy—essential to any true portrayal of the human condition—are simply misled by the understandable Christian tendency to avoid the tragedy of the story of Jesus, and indeed of the human condition as such, by talking of death as if we *knew* that his death, and ours, was just a staging post on the way to the glorious victory.

Perhaps the Christian story itself misleads us here—for stories of their nature have sequences, and the literal-minded tend to take them as the plainest of plain history. Death then becomes an entry on a calendar rather than, as Heidegger knew, a definitive condition of There-being, and resurrection becomes another entry sometime later; and although we don't know the exact date of the second entry (as Jesus *did*), we can in his case and ours pass quickly over the first regrettable entry and go on virtually unscathed to the second. The only death we then need to record is the death of tragedy, and the death of all verisimilitude. Our story now is not in the least lifelike, and somewhere deep down we all know that perfectly well. Paul's fear that the cross of Christ might be 'emptied of its power' (1 Cor. 1: 17) was not fanciful. On this literal-minded reading of the Christian sources the cross is just a failure, to be succeeded and suppressed, as quickly as possible by another quite different event called the resurrection and marked 'success'; and it is this latter event which provides the power to live.

But no: the victory over death, the victory known as resurrection, must be in life, just as death is in Everyman's life and in every part of it. The Christian conviction is that victory over death in life is achieved by a kind of dying. Hence Jesus' paradoxical teaching: to lose life is to gain it.

But paradoxes are too often substitutes for hard thinking, and so we must say what this one means. As is usual in Christianity, true participation in true Eucharist makes meanings much plainer than mere verbal analysis could ever do—though we are here inevitably confined to mere verbal analysis of true Eucharist!

It is only too obvious that most ways of losing and taking life gain nothing at all except death, for involved and uninvolved alike. So what is this way of losing life that can record a gain for life? The clue is contained in the first action of the Eucharistic drama: to take as gift (*gratia*), to hold in gratitude (*gratias agere*); for this means, in the words of Gerard Manley Hopkins, to keep grace that keeps all one's goings graces. What is held as gift, be it life itself, is held in permanent openness, to be broken, poured out again in gift. This is the way with life that preserves in faith, as Heidegger would say; in a practical faith that at the heart of reality is goodness overflowing, *diffusivum sui*, poured out over and over again. Such dying for life is a feature of every act of grace, of every gracious gesture. In the impetuous generosity of the lesser kinds of loving—the kind, for instance, that in retrospect was no more than youthful infatuation—something of the paradoxical self-fulfilment of selflessness, something of the joy of higher kinds of loving, is already experienced. But it is of course in the case of the ultimate human *gratia*, the gracious gesture of giving life itself as the price of fidelity or the ransom for others, whether that is a continous gesture over time or a final grand gesture at a life's end, that the higher, fuller life is finally touched which for a Christian is the divine life. Grace, love (at least a certain kind of loving), joy, are but verbal reeds which can bend and show where this distinctive spirit blows.

Eucharist, then, in Paul's words, proclaims the death of Jesus, for Christians look for divinity present, not in an abstract Feuerbachian human nature, but in a dying Jew. The Eucharistic prayer of Hippolytus had the celebrants say that in the Eucharist they performed the *anamnesis* of Jesus' death *and* resurrection. But the addition was really unnecessary. The way of Jesus' living and dying was his rising. He was indeed Risen/Lord, to those who could take it, during his life, and never more so than in his consummate death.

As a matter of fact, that phrase 'to those who could take it' gives the clue to the only answer we may give to the stubborn and persistent question: but what did happen to Jesus, then, after his death?

## The continuing presence of the body of Jesus in the world

Because of the dualism which has somehow come to infect traditional christology we tend to think separately of Jesus' divinity and of Jesus' humanity. Since divinity is commonly thought to be safe from death, we persist in wanting to know what happened after death to Jesus' 'human nature'? The original Christian story, however, knows nothing of such dualism, nothing of such separable fates. The story tells of a spirit which came upon Jesus; in one version of the story it came upon his mother at his conception. It tells of a power, of a life which it believes to be divine, which broke into human history in definitive form as Jesus of Nazareth. The fate of Jesus, which the story describes as his lordship, is therefore inseparably bound to the fate of this spirit in the world. Eucharist, which is the occasion *par excellence* for encounter with the real presence of this spirit in the world, is also therefore the occasion on which one can best assess its fate. If this spirit can be seen to fashion the body of Christ as it once 'inspired' the life and death of Jesus, then Jesus is both Christ and Lord; then Jesus is indeed risen. But if the adversary power of flesh, if the satanic spirit which tries to live by killing rather than live by dying, is seen to prevail at Eucharist, then the conclusion must be that Jesus is to that extent not raised.

It is important not to attempt to shirk this further implication of the insight that Eucharist is the resurrection/appearances of the Risen/Lord. Nor should it come as any surprise to any reader of early eucharistic prayers and early eucharistic theology to find that such implication was at times explicitly drawn, for this early Christian doctrine is characterized precisely by the use of the imagery of spirit to draw together the themes of incarnation, resurrection, and Eucharist. So, for example, an early Eucharistic prayer from a document known as the *Testamentum Domini*, the Covenant of the Lord, contains the words: 'When you shall do this, you shall make my resurrection'; and one of Theodore of Mopsuestia's comments on the Eucharistic *epiclesis* reads: 'it is necessary, therefore, that our Lord should now rise from the dead by the power of the things which are taking place'.[2] It is perfectly clear that if we do not do 'this', if the 'things which are taking place' are the opposite, if only in intent, of the symbolic taking and breaking and giving, then Jesus is not rising from the dead; death is keeping its frozen grip upon his body, and keeping his life-giving spirit entombed in the resulting corpse of Christ. More detailed examples can come later; but if Christians refuse to break bread at the table of the Lord even with other Christians it is clear that the spirit of reconciliation is being smothered alive, and that no eucharistic theology or theory of eucharistic presidency can compensate for the deadly damage that thereby continues to be done to the crippled body of Christ.

The final implication of the insight that Eucharist is resurrection/appearances can be drawn by the simple strategy of recalling that the point of proclaiming resurrection is to proclaim divinity. The final implication is this: if the fate of Jesus is inseparable from the sojourn of his body in the world, so is the fate of God. And that leads us back once more to the beginning, to the God-question as it is called. One can say it again: the most serious and unavoidable issue for every human being is not the theoretical question, does God exist? This can be answered in one way or another by flights of reasoning, all of which soon leave the common ground of our day-to-day existence far behind.

Traditional arguments for God's existence do begin from such common ground—from the ambivalence of change with its ubiquitous threat and promise, from the power and process of causal efficacy, from the stark contingency of things and their essential time-conditionedness, from the order that so precariously and with such huge expense of unrelenting effort survives the encroaching chaos, from the beauty which can always be glimpsed through the ugliness that is the embodiment of death.

Perhaps it was the original intent of these traditional arguments simply to point to these features of our world as the occasions for some form of faith. Perhaps the point of that strange argument known as the Ontological Argument was to convince us that we already knew what we could on these occasions come to believe. Yet the traditional treatment of all these arguments led away from experience, up longer and longer ladders of logic to ever more rarified conclusions.

The most serious problem we face is that of discerning the powers by which our destinies are decided, in the hope of encountering the one that can sustain our highest hopes. Christians point to Jesus and to the continuing presence of his body in the world, and they point in particular to the Eucharist as the occasion on which this ultimate power can be encountered. Now it is impossible to talk about God without talking about totality, or about what is called creation. For creation is not a question of remote beginnings such as physicists might discuss. It is about the innermost power of being by which it is, by which it erupts, by which it sustains itself against nothingness; it is about the character of this power and hence about the innermost character of all that is.

Eucharist involves the commonest of food and one of the commonest and most basic of human activities, eating and drinking. It is a meal—not any designated category of meal, a Passover meal or some sort of sacred meal, just a meal. But its ritual of taking thankfully and breaking to give to others is symbolic, by the kind of spirit it makes present, of the character of God, and hence of the innermost power of all reality. It tells of God by capturing the inner power of divine creation, by inaugurating those relations of grace which prefigure the future of God and the goal of all creation, freed at last from the enslavement under which the whole of creation groans. This larger point was reached in early Christian doctrine by the use of the imagery of spirit to draw together the themes of incarnation, resurrection, Eucharist, *and* creation, when the divine spirit brooded on the abyss. But perhaps the point is more accessible to a modern mind through Evelyn Underhill's poem, 'Corpus Christi':

Come, dear Heart!
The fields are white to harvest: come and see
As in a glass the timeless mystery
Of love, whereby we feed
On God, our bread indeed.
Torn by the sickles, see him share the smart
Of travailing Creation: maimed, despised,
Yet by his lovers the more dearly prized
Because for us he lays his beauty down—
Last toll paid by Perfection for our loss!
Trace on these fields his everlasting Cross,
And o'er the stricken sheaves the Immortal Victim's crown.

From far horizons came a Voice that said,
'Lo! from the hand of Death take thou thy daily bread.'
Then I, awakening, saw
A splendour burning in the heart of things:
The flame of living love which lights the law
Of mystic death that works the mystic birth.
I knew the patient passion of the earth,
Maternal, everlasting, whence there springs
The Bread of Angels and the life of man.
Now in each blade
I, blind no longer, see
The glory of God's growth: know it to be
An earnest of the Immemorial Plan.
Yea, I have understood
How all things are one great oblation made:
He on our altars, we on the world's rood.
Even as this corn,
Earth-born,
We are snatched from the sod,
Reaped, ground to grist,
Crushed and tormented in the Mills of God,
And offered at Life's hands, a living Eucharist.

Marx was quite right to say that it is in praxis, the truth that is
done, that the truth about the world is best known. Eucharistic
praxis attempts to establish the correct active relationship of
human beings with the world from which they most immediately
sustain their life. This relationship we can describe as 'relations

of grace' within the Marxist 'relations of production'; for the relationship fashioned in the Eucharist is that between the recipient and a gift freely given (the original meaning of the word 'grace', which then by extension came to mean thanksgiving). The relationship entails on the side of the gift a brokenness and a pouring out, and on the side of the recipient a corresponding openness. But Eucharist is *symbolic* praxis, which means that it is effective only if this relationship spreads out beyond the celebration. The point of claiming that in Eucharist one encounters no less than the true God, then, is to say that only if this relationship spreads to the whole of creation will the true God be encountered. This is the point that early Christian theology covered explicitly by depicting the same spirit in creation as in incarnation, resurrection, and Eucharist. The spirit that one breathes in the eucharistic celebration is the spirit that came upon creation, according to the first creation myth in the Book of Genesis.

From the truth of this distinctive praxis derives the specifically Christian doctrine of creation. When early Christian theologians said that the same spirit which breathed in the Eucharist brooded over creation they had effectively reformulated the Genesis myth, for the spirit that *they* were talking about was the spirit Jesus breathed as he died. Paul had already accomplished an equally radical rewriting of Scripture when he identified the Word by which all things were made with the crucified Jew, wrote of the Word of the Cross (1 Cor. 1: 18), and then proceeded to name the crucified Jew 'the Power of God and the Wisdom of God'.

The symbolic praxis of the Eucharist attempts to convey the truth that the spirit which definitively entered human history as Jesus of Nazareth is nothing less than the power of God and the secret character of God's creation. The divinity of Jesus is thus experienced, true divinity is encountered, by those who recognize the character of things by which they are grace poured out, broken, and given to all. And God is encountered as creator in this experience, not because he utters an invulnerable word which by overwhelming power makes all things just what he wills them to be; creation is a matter of giving things and giving them up so that they, by giving themselves again, can seek the source of grace.

The spirit of God is at risk in creation, suffering creation's sacrifice and its reverses. If Christians who refuse to break bread with each other keep the stone at the opening of Jesus' tomb, then all who refuse to allow bread to be broken to the hungry of this world pile their food mountains over the grave of God.

It is a mistake to ask about the fate of Jesus' humanity 'after his death' and in contradistinction to the fate of his divinity. If one reads the Eucharist rightly God's fate is bound up with that of Jesus and of his body in the world, and so the fate of all is bound up with God's. We are to be a 'spiritual body', in Paul's language, and that means the body of God. We have some experience of what that can mean in life and in death; we have no picture of what it means beyond our individual deaths. The ultimate giving up hides the ultimate depth of what the penumbra of death allows us to experience of the surprising enrichment of self-sacrificing love. Meanwhile in present Eucharistic experience the body of Christ is still trying to break loose from the bonds of death in this world, and not yet succeeding, and God still seeks to be God through Jesus Christ whom his followers with their lips confess to be Lord.

# 4

# The Way (iii): The Life of Jesus

What was it about Jesus that made it at all feasible for people to point to the presence of ultimate power or spirit? What could possibly have made them claim that Jesus himself was raised, exalted to lordship, divine? One answer, if it can be found, will satisfy both questions. This is because, in his efforts to enable people to encounter God, Jesus did not point away from himself. He never quite behaved as a middleman, the bearer of a revelation which God had deposited in him for transmission through the spoken or written word. He never pointed to something in this world other than himself which was to be the privileged locus for the encounter with divine spirit. Neither of course did he spend his time pointing to himself, at least not in the form of making claims concerning his person. His consuming passion was the reign of God, not the role or the status of Jesus of Nazareth.

Yet he acted with and towards others, and it was in these actions that he gave them to understand how the one true God could be encountered. His speech was typically a call to join in the action, and sometimes an explanation or a justification of it. In fact, the most characteristic of his speech-forms, the parable, is inherently dramatic. Related as it is to poetry through the common blood of metaphor, parable actually evokes an experience and involves a person. Parable is to speech what ritual is to action; it is sacramental; it lures into action. Indeed it sometimes goads into kinds of action which are quite the opposite of what Jesus intended, but opposition too has its own way of sharply illustrating what Jesus tried to achieve. And so it was in the imaginative praxis of Jesus that what he called the reign of God was to be encountered. And so it is that for Christians the presence of ultimate power has always been inseparable from the powerful presence of Jesus. Those who thought Jesus wrong could never be satisfied to point out that he was mistaken, as it is always possible to do with someone who simply transmits a message or interprets a previous revelation. It was necessary at the very least to accuse him of blasphemy, and at best to declare that the spirit which inspired him was Beelzebub. He was either Beelzebub in the flesh or God's spirit in the flesh; his preference for going into action in the way that he did left his onlookers no other option.

What was it then that made it at all feasible for people to point to Jesus as the presence of ultimate power, and in this way to claim that Jesus was exalted by God to lordship, that he was in fact divine? Everything that has been said about history and faith, and about imagination and praxis, would lead one to look for the answer to this question in the humanity of Jesus. The primacy of imagination and of the way that it works prevents any initial separation of God from creation. It is the later analytic activity of the mind that makes God distant and therefore intellectually understandable. The kingdom, the power and the glory must first be sought, as Jesus said, amongst or even within us. The human creature, Jesus of Nazareth, accepted as such without any qualification, is where we start; not with any presence beside or behind him, betrayed by kinds of action which could not be human.

History makes the same point. Any action performed by a human being is by definition a human act. The only question for history is whether it did or did not occur. And faith on any thorough analysis of it concurs. Any event in which God might be claimed to be present is in our preception of it finite; any claim that God is present to us, all biblical claims included, must come from human claimants; any conviction that any claim concerning God's presence in any event is in fact true is first perceived as a human conviction, and *its* divine origin, if such is claimed, is a further instance of human claim and conviction. There is no escape, this side of death at least, from the skin of human faith in which we dance our lives away. We must begin with Jesus, a man like us in all things—except, it is claimed, that he did not sin. The various titles were added later, the illuminating promise of each always accompanied by the restriction of its vision. But first to appear in the opening scene on the undistinguished stage of ancient Galilee was just a man. Not a 'mere' man, as if something should immediately be added, whatever this might be, to make him more than mere. If the life of Jesus proved anything at all, it proved that the adjective 'mere' is inapplicable to human kind. But then it does not take the life of Jesus to prove that. A true artist can evoke the still unfathomed depths of humanity, and few artists have done this as powerfully as Samuel Beckett. Relentlessly reduced to immobility and silence, Beckett's characters project, with unbearable poignancy, the irreducible dignity of our kind, a native dignity that is not based on social endowment or personal achievement but on some indefinable human potential to meet the inevitable tragedy of existence.

## Jesus' arrival in the world

Jesus, too, was at first a most ordinary man, and it is extremely important to say so. His origins were obscure in the extreme. It is difficult to be sure even about the place of his birth. The genealogies which Luke and Matthew offer allow little possibility of proving that he was of royal lineage; the title 'son of David' belongs to a later theological confession. We know nothing to distinguish his family tree from that of any other poor person. Obscure origins are, of course, always vulnerable in innuendo, and it seems likely that some of Jesus' opponents later said that he was an illegitimate child. Villagers in particular will know what a poor defence it would be to say in answer to such an accusation that the Holy Spirit had had a hand in the matter. And it is widely accepted that the point of the nativity stories, which differ so remarkably in detail between Matthew and Luke, was not in the main to provide this poor defence.

Raymond Brown's *Birth of the Messiah* is perhaps the most complete study of these stories to date. Brown tends to err, if he does err, on the conservative side. He believes that a combination of historical evidence and argument from likelihoods favours virginal conception over illegitimacy, and that a third possibility of Joseph's parentage is not in contention. But Brown is as adamant as anyone that the principal point of the nativity stories is to establish the presence of the divine spirit at the very conception of

Jesus and the corresponding confession that he was Son of God. All are agreed that it is not virginal conception that makes one Son of God, or even tells one what that title might mean, just as it is not revival of a corpse that makes its owner Son of God—and Brown is at his theological best in showing how these themes of spirit and sonship recur in nativity stories, in resurrection preaching, and as we must shortly see, in the stories about Jesus' baptism.

There is then nothing that we can discover about Jesus' arrival on the human scene that would enable us to use the title Son of God of him, or tell us what we meant if we did so (for the title was used at the time of different types of people). The only thing we can assume to have been unusual about the circumstances of his birth—for obscurity is not all that unusual—is the very thing that left him open to accusations of illegitimacy. That of course aligned him with a subset of human beings much maligned in most cultures—but then Jesus would often in his life be aligned with the most marginalized of his fellows. He was a most ordinary man.

Our opening question is not only still intact; it becomes more pressing. What could possibly lead anyone to claim that divine spirit lived the life of this obscure and vulnerable individual? The next event in his life to which we have any substantial reference is his baptism in the Jordan by John the Baptist. It is scarcely possible to say now with any certainty whether or not he was at first a follower of John's. The scriptural accounts of the incident are anxious to stress, for reasons which will eventually give us the answer to our question, his superiority to John. Yet they cannot forget, and they do not care to deny, that Jesus did go down to the Jordan to be baptized in a ritual cleansing which Mark explicitly describes as a baptism of repentance for the forgiveness of sins (Mark 1: 4). He is now to be found amongst those who came to John the Baptist, in a common crowd of self-confessed sinners. Yet again divine spirit is declared to be present in this ordinary event, and the declaration that Jesus is in this the Son of God is attributed by Luke to a voice from heaven (Luke 3: 22). The story of Jesus in its earliest incidents continues to be a story of ordinary things, the only unusual features of the story being those which so consistently align him with outcasts and sinners. Yet it is claimed that his spirit was divine, that he was Son of God. Why?

In his public life, as it is called, Jesus did not have the valuable backing of belonging to some recognized vocation or profession. In a sense the efforts of modern scholars to decide about his contemporary classification bear a marked resemblance to efforts to give him his proper title after his death. Was he, as Geza Vermes thinks, one of those miracle-working holy men from Galilee, a member of the Hasidim, or, as Reginald Fuller would prefer, a prophet, or a wandering rabbi, as Bultmann believes the historical evidence suggests? The trouble with these categories is the same as the trouble with all the titles which have since been conferred upon him. They do less to explain him than he does to break open all the established imagery by which they had domesticated the highest of human expectations. He had no visible source of authority such as society then or now could recognize for doing what he did. The scandal of the cross is adumbrated from his very conception. He was a man, and furthermore one whose name was linked with those to whom we should be least inclined to go for anything that we might want. A far too ordinary man. It was a man, just a man, that was divine power incarnate.

Was Feuerbach right then in identifying divinity with humanity? Leaving aside altogether the way in which he fell foul of Marx's criticism, no, he was not. For Feuerbach, in spite of all his insistence on human transcendence, does try to define man, and in this way he reduces God. The quester after divine incarnation must try to look through the perpetual openness of human transcendence into the indefinable depth of God. Well, was Marx right then in his vision of a more concrete human future, created without a God? That remains to be seen. The human future for Marx depended upon that praxis which both results from and constitutes transformed relations of production. Everything now depends upon Jesus' praxis, upon the kind of relations which it reveals and fashions, upon the hopes to which these relations can lead. For this one must inspect his public mission.

## Jesus' public mission

Few things are as certain about the historical Jesus as the title he gave to the cause to which he devoted his life. The first public pronouncement which Mark places on the lips of Jesus reads somewhat as follows: the time is ripe, the kingdom of God is at hand, prepare for a complete change of heart and believe this good news.

The kingdom of God was the name of the cause, but what did that mean? Well, at the very least it meant that whatever was to come about was to be attributed to God and not to any other agency—although, like everything else that is attributed to God in the world, it was also expected to come about through what the philosophers call secondary causes, in this case with human co-operation. Beyond that the meaning depends upon the speaker, and in particular on the kind of activity in which he engaged and which *he* at least took to be co-operation in the coming of the kingdom. This may sound disappointingly inconclusive, but it could scarcely be otherwise with a symbol which had such deep roots in the ancient memory of Israel. Israel had been chosen by God of old, and at its best Israel believed that it was chosen not for itself but for the whole world and for its total future. Israel's destiny was thus under the sovereignty of God, and through Israel the destiny of the world. However, the sheer extent and variety of Israel's historic experience had inevitably by the time of Jesus given rise to different ways of imagining God's rule for the future. And the resulting variety is not altogether a disadvantage, for it is partly by differentiating that we learn to identify things, and there is ample evidence to suggest that Jesus was not loath to press his interpretation of the reign of God upon representatives of rival views.

## *Rival interpretations of the reign of God in Jesus' time*

Let us first look briefly at the most politically radical interpretation of the symbol, the reign of God, in the age of Jesus. Josephus in his *Jewish Antiquities* called it the Fourth Philosophy, because he placed the three other major interpretations of the time before it. But so many people seem so determined to persuade us that the cause of Jesus was religious rather than political—as if it had ever been possible to keep these altogether separate—and so to prevent us, however unwittingly, from giving an account of the life of Jesus adequate to explain his execution as a state criminal, that we might insist on looking first in this direction and let the last, for once, be first.

Josephus describes the Jewish Fourth Philosophy in terms largely reminiscent of contemporary Cynic thought. The people who put forward this philosophy acknowledged no lord or master other than God. Mastery over others, of course, then as now depended upon unequal access to wealth in whatever form or forms it might take at any particular time. So it is not surprising that the determination to offer allegiance to God alone should be accompanied by a resistance to the payment of taxes to Caesar and to the taking of a census, which itself was largely for taxation purposes. The Fourth Philosophy did not necessarily entail armed resistance, so the people who proposed it cannot be described without more ado as Zealots. Recourse to armed violence is seldom the prerogative of any particular party in political affairs—and around the time of Jesus supporters of at least two of the other philosophies showed as much enthusiasm for armed insurrection as any of the Zealots.

Josephus describes the exponents of the Fourth Philosophy as 'sowing the seeds of civil strife', but the followers of all the philosophies retained in their communal memory the image of Yahweh, Lord of Hosts, the old warlord who destroyed whole armies in the course of the constitutional liberation from Egyptian slavery, and who bade his armies wipe out whole peoples in order to conquer the territory which he thus 'gave' them. In the Temple, the spiritual heart of the nation, the great annual cultic dramas continued the *anamnesis* of Yahweh's mighty deeds in favour of his chosen people. When violence did finally erupt after AD 66 the radical activists of the Fourth Philosophy, together with members of other parties equally zealous for Yahweh's sole lordship, all Zealots now, fought their way to the inner Temple, there expecting God's intervention to crown their efforts to inaugurate his kingdom. Christian commentators on the New Testament often urge us to say 'rule of God' rather than 'kingdom of God' so as to avoid all insinuation of territorial intent, but it is clear that the symbol could come to involve territorial claims just as easily as it could be commandeered by the military.

Armed insurrection was even less essential to the philosophy of the Pharisee party, as it came to be called, than it was to the exponents of the Fourth Philosophy. The Pharisees seem to have looked to the Temple and to the ritual purity of its priesthood for their main model of the kind of behaviour which would bring the reign of God—a natural move for those who thought Yahweh particularly present in his Temple. And if priestly activities in the Temple were thought in consequence to be the principal means of contact with God, then the sacerdotalizing of secular life, to the extent that this could be achieved, would seem an obvious formula for the extension of Yahweh's reign, and one moreover which would work if, by some great disaster, the Temple were no longer to exist. The nation itself, in words from an inspired Christian author, could be 'a holy priesthood', 'a royal priesthood' (1 Pet. 2: 5, 9).

The philosophy of the Qumran community seems to have been based on the belief that compromise was endemic to the city, and that the only way to achieve a purified community in anticipation of God's final rule was to withdraw to the monastic enclaves, preferably of desert places.

Finally, the Sadducee party, conservative and fundamentalist in its theology, confining divine revelation to the 'five books of Moses', felt free to exercise for the good of the people whatever delegated power the Roman overlords were prepared to allow in a subjugate territory.

Jesus did not retire to a monastery. Like the wandering teachers—indeed preachers of the Cynic philosophy—he took his cause to the street corners. Nor had he any natural entrée into the Sadducee party: he was neither a priest nor a member of one of the aristocratic families. In fact it was probably members of this party that helped persuade the Roman governor to execute him in the end. It is really in the differences and similarities between his cause and those of the Pharisees and of the Fourth Philosophy that the distinctiveness of Jesus' interpretation of the rule of God is to be found. The more specific question of his attitude to armed violence, on the other hand, must be raised in conjunction with all four rival philosophies, since arms provide an option at some stage for all of them.

## Jesus and the reign of God: His practice of table-fellowship

When Jesus went public, then, and proclaimed to a country well used to hearing it that the kingdom of God was at hand, how did it dawn on his listeners that he envisaged yet a different reign and, to that extent, a somewhat different God? And how did they come to realize that the reign he envisaged was so different that none of the major parties would offer him any substantial support, while some of them actually contrived with the Romans to have him executed as a messianic pretender between two premature Zealots? I am fully persuaded by the American New Testament scholar, Norman Perrin, that any effort to answer these questions should first involve looking to Jesus' practice of table-fellowship, the one unique ritual left to his followers to continue after his death.

Every table is in a very real way an altar. Reduced to the level of biological necessity, the intake of food and drink for the purpose of fuelling and lubricating the body-machine could be achieved by swift and solitary ingestion. The fast-food phenomenon provides one of the most startling illustrations of what a scientific, technological age can do to a culture. For every known culture engages in the extraordinary ritual of teaching its young to offer to others at table the food and drink which they instinctively know they need for life itself, and to wait upon the outstretched hands of others, upon open, chaliced hands, for their own essential sustenance. Every meal is a sacrifice, its symbolism potentially powerful and, up to recent times, quite universal. Those who argue as to whether a meal, any meal, is either a sacrifice or a sacrament have somehow managed to unlearn a lesson which any culture could teach them: that every meal is sacrifice in symbolic or sacramental form.

The quest for the divine has never to the best of our knowledge received aid from the divinity in the form of special 'divine' symbols, verbal or other, for the description of divinity or of its alleged behaviour. People use whatever words they have to say what they can about power and presence, and they choose from among their activities those most suitable for symbolizing such heights and depths of their experience as raise the hopes and fears of the divine. Words which refer to the surprising and threatened fact that we and the things around us exist at all are most suitable; and so is that activity on which the continuance of life depends as it depends on no other. Meals are at the heart of the rituals of most, if not all, religions. The meal, more so perhaps than the act of breathing from which the imagery of God as life-giving spirit/breath derives, is to religious ritual what the language of to be or not to be is to religious language.

'On this mountain the Lord of hosts will make for all peoples a feast of fat things.' So said Isaiah (25: 6). Israel made its own characteristic use of the ritual and symbolism of the meal, and since the kingship of Yahweh was central both in Jewish history and in the earliest known Jewish prayers the use of the meal symbolism to celebrate the kingship was inevitable. In one sense, explicit evidence of people linking meals and kingship is as unnecessary as is explicit evidence of the use of the actual phrase 'the kingdom of God'. Just as the use of Jesus' favourite symbol is implicit in all the psalms and prayers that addressed Yahweh as king, so the use of the meal to celebrate Yahweh's rule, even in anticipation, is already indicated in the ancient Near Eastern image of the king as the one who feeds his people.

We may not have any explicit evidence that the Pharisees of Jesus' time used the phrase 'the kingdom of God', and they may even have avoided it because of the militaristic overtones which others gave it—our Christian sources show how prone Jesus' followers were to misunderstand his use of the phrase in that particular way. But we do know that before the failed insurrection and the destruction of the Temple in AD 70 the Pharisees did practise table-fellowship with the purity of Temple practice, and believed that they followed the law of God. After all, at the end of the Lord's Prayer we use the terms kingdom, power, and glory of God as the equivalents which they are. Pharisees would have well understood that in the meal one could encounter God's power, and the glory which in other views was confined to the innermost

Temple. We know, too, that the messianic banquet, the meal to symbolize and to celebrate the final rule of God's anointed one, was familiar to the Qumran party. Isaiah's imagery is well attested at the time of Jesus, and its connection with the symbolism of God's reign sufficiently obvious to support fully Perrin's contention that it was Jesus' practice of table-fellowship that mainly drew the attention and the hostility of other parties. But what was distinctive about Jesus' table-fellowship, and what did it reveal about his particular understanding of God's ways with the world?

This question is answered at the beginning of the earliest of the gospels, that of Mark, through the words of representatives of a rival interpretation of God's ways with the world, the Pharisees. 'Why', they ask, 'does he eat with tax-collectors and sinners?' (Mark 2: 16). Matthew has Jesus himself attribute this same complaint more broadly to 'this generation': 'the son of man came eating and drinking, and they say, "Behold, a glutton and a drunkard, a friend of tax-collectors and sinners" ' (Matt. 11: 19). It was the openness of his table that was seen to be distinctive of the meals in which Jesus gave people to understand the rule and power of God could be encountered, and it was this which aroused their opposition. All the native power of the symbolism of sharing one's food with another, all the added religious symbolism which allows a meal to make claims about God, all the well-directed force of *Jewish* symbolic meals which symbolized God's *Jewish* ways with the world, built up behind this opposition until it finally destroyed the man who in any case had no table of his own.

Tax-collectors and sinners—a laundry-bag phrase that! An all-embracing phrase for the figures who shuffle through the gospels like the figures in Beckett's *Quad I and II*, always missing the centre of the mandala and losing their battle with time, the prodigal, the Samaritan, the prostitute, the dishonest, the unclean, all the people with whom for reasons racial and moral, religious and economic, political and historical, one does not share one's food—and most particularly not in such a context as would suggest that God without more ado on their part extended his generosity to them, that his rain refreshed the good and the evil alike, that his sun warmed equally the just and the unjust. This breaking of bread was unconditional forgiveness not in jejune declaratory form, but in the enriching and inspiring form of grace, for grace simply means a gift freely given, and food shared is the most fundamental of gifts. Jesus did declare in words God's unconditional forgiveness, and the offence was increased by his stubbornness on the issue, but the real source of the offence was the gracious action. Without the action the words might have been excused as a mistaken interpretation of some difficult Scripture. The symbolic power of the meal was pivotal. A saying which Matthew attributes to Jesus echoes the universalism of the text from Isaiah: 'I tell you, many will come from east and west and sit at table with Abraham, Isaac and Jacob in the kingdom of heaven' (Matt. 8: 11). There was no mistaking the radical force of this latest interpretation of the reign of God, and its offensiveness was merely increased by its appropriating to itself the universalist themes of Israel's most generous moods.

Readers of the magisterial Book of Job will know that conventional wisdom connected suffering with sin, and so expected that the relief of suffering of all kinds should follow the final forgiveness of sins. Jesus, like Job, dissented from the straightforward connection of suffering and sin (Luke 13: 1–5), while allowing that the continued refusal by human beings of a complete change of heart threatened all with ultimate destruction. He thus did not altogether disappoint those who felt that a rule of God which was so commonly expressed in terms of forgiveness should also result in the relief of suffering. But by refusing a simple punitive account of suffering and a consequently legalistic expectation of its relief, he opted, as John's gospel (9: 3) shows, for the positive causal link between relief of human suffering and the in-breaking reign of God, 'the works of God made manifest' as John puts it. According to Jesus' interpretation the reign of God would heal human ills; the fullest symbolism of the sharing of food would be realized, and so forgiveness would continue to take the positive, creative form of grace, rather than the more negative form of simply declaring trespasses forgotten. The blind see, the lame walk, lepers are cleansed, the hungry are fed—gracious action continues to be the primary source of the experience of the reign of God in the life of Jesus.

An ordinary man at ordinary meals was beginning to look quite extraordinary. Because he harnessed the powerful traditional religious symbolism of the final rule of God to the grace of shared food at ordinary meals in ordinary houses? Probably not; his co-religionists could probably accept this building upon the native symbolism of the meal. What they could not accept was the unlimited, unconditional, in their eyes indiscriminate extension of the gift of bread, the grace of drink, to those who for whatever reason had found or placed themselves outside the reach of God's favour and who, in everyone else's view of the matter, needed to take some standard steps to come within it. Dramatic symbols—or sacraments as they are called—allow an initial participation in the kind of thing which they symbolize. This man was prepared to follow through fully the symbol of sharing bread and drink as the giving of life: he was prepared to serve particularly wherever life was reduced by need or suffering and to serve the outcasts as much as those thought deserving of it, the unclean and all those whom respectable society had shut off from itself by walls of stone or the more impenetrable walls of guilt and fear and prejudice. In Matthew's great judgement scene the damned are told that they did not feed the hungry, give drink to the thirsty, clothe the naked, welcome the stranger, or visit the sick and those in prison. There is no mention of having a fasle theology of the Eucharist or of losing the apostolic succession.

The full relevance to Jesus' own interpretation of the rule of God of his healing and feeding has always been clouded by one or other of the following factors. At first his inclusion of the outcasts of society produced the expected sense of outrage. Later, in centuries which considered themselves more sophisticated, it was the description of so much of this activity as exorcism that invited a cultured rejection—and few things are as sure about the historical Jesus as the fact that he did perform as an exorcist. But if spirit and power could be virtual synonyms for God's rule, as indeed they were, there is no cogent reason why the kind of destructive power of evil in the world which at every pass obstructs the benign spirit of God should not, whatever its presumed origin, be thought and named a spirit, an adversary, Satan.

Whether such names are to be counted as personification or hypostatization, and just how naïve they may be considered to be, is rather incidental in the present context, and may safely be relegated to other places in theology where personification is discussed. It is clear from Jesus' practice that the spirit and power of the in-breaking rule of God had to counter all adversary spirit and contrary power which diminished human life and gave to human death its terrible sting.

Finally, it was also in soi-disant sophisticated centuries that Jesus' service to the suffering was dumped indiscriminately into the category of the miraculous. Its original point was then lost in wearisome debates as to what, if anything, might prove to be a miracle and what, if anything, a miracle might prove. Now there is no doubt that the New Testament makes very conventional use of conventional types of miracle story, and philosophical and theological discussions of miracle stories have their value. But for our purpose at this point it is the familiar New Testament description of these acts of service to the suffering as *dunameis*, deeds of power, that is paramount. It is this description that tells the discriminating reader that in Jesus' understanding of the matter the reign of God erupts in such service and that such service defines the kingdom. The healing of those injured by the power of evil constitutes deeds of the kingdom, of the power, of the glory; it is the reign of God in action as Jesus interprets the reign of God.

## *Jesus and the reign of God: His prayer and his parables*

When we come to the words in which Jesus evoked his distinctive experience of the reign of God, mention must first be made of his prayer, for prayer is a particularly powerful form of human utterance. Rising from a depth of the human spirit at which belief and unbelief have not yet parted, nearer to the fathomless nature of naked hope than to the surface of settled convictions, accessible alike to atheist and theist, prayer asks for what it has and seeks to understand what it knows. As a form of utterance it therefore comes closest to expressing in clear words or incoherent groans the primordial conditions of all human existence, which is in question to its very core, and always in quest of some answering god. Jesus' prayer is summarized most succinctly by Luke: 'Father, hallowed be thy name. Thy kingdom come. Give us each day our daily bread; and forgive us our sins, for we ourselves forgive everyone who is indebted to us; and lead us not into temptation' (Luke 11: 2-4).

'Father' is part of the prayer, not just the name of the one to whom it is addressed, not a character of God which, even if we knew what kind of fatherhood is meant, could simply be assumed. Father is not a common name for God in the Original Testament; it is there confined to material which concerns either the exodus from Egypt or the rise of the Davidic dynasty. It is, therefore, like the kingdom which is the next object of the prayer, something we shall know when we experience it, if we ever can experience it. In the form of an explicit question, rather than the spiritual groping of prayer, the question, what does divine father-hood mean, is quite similar to the question, what is the kingdom of God in Jesus' version of it? And it must be answered in the same way: through active commitment deeply penetrated by imagination; in short, through praxis. It is therefore significant that the very next phrase brings us back to the meal: give us each day our daily bread. Are we asking God to supply more cereal? No. True prayer is not petitionary in that way. Mark gives no version of the Lord's Prayer but a passage in his gospel is a good gloss on it (Mark 11: 22-6): 'I tell you, whatever you ask in prayer, believe that you have received it, and it will be yours.' Odd, is it not, that combination of tenses? But is there a better way of suggesting that what is at issue in a rule or a fatherhood which might be considered divine is not an extra being nor any extra thing, but a new active relation to what there already is as part of a new way of imagining it, the same new way which the eucharistic action invokes when it asks us to take with thanks as gift or grace what is already there, to break and give; a relation of grace, one might say, that is prior to relations of production?

And *then* come the phrases about forgiveness, because our forgiveness of others is already there in the sharing of our bread with them, as God's forgiveness is already in the bread, the wheat, the soil, and, as Jesus once suggested, in the sheer exuber-ant indiscriminacy of sun and rain. The prayer ends with some peremptory words about a temptation, or better still a test or trial. These words refer back to the inherently sacrificial nature of every meal-ritual, and to the unrestricted range of its symbolism. If you break and give your bread, you may one day give your life. This last 'petition' of the prayer corresponds rather significantly with the last meal, the Last Supper, in which the imagery of self-sacrifice is now made explicit, in face of imminent death, in the words over the bread and the cup. In fact Matthew's characteristic doubling of the last 'petition' makes it seem more realistic than it is in Luke's version, for whereas Luke's version just might suggest that sacrifice is avoidable, Matthew adds 'but deliver us from evil'. Sacrifice is essential to this way; it is deliverance that can be in doubt for those whose faith can be shaken. So the form of the very same prayer which Jesus prays in Gethsemane puts deliverance first.

Yet it is of crucial importance not to separate sacrifice and deliverance, the first to be undergone as quietly as possible, teeth clenched, the second to be expected as soon as possible. Such lines of thought mistake the way of Jesus, mistake the symbolism of the meal, and end in a separation of resurrection and crucifixion which threatens the true Christian understanding of both. The meals of Jesus were joyful—we know that from his use of the symbol of the bridgegroom, and from the jibe about gluttons and drunkards—for the deepest joy is in the breaking and the pouring out, just as a grace is never more a grace than when it is given again. And so it is right that when we come to Jesus' other verbal ways of invoking his unique experience of the reign of God, the parables, we should let the note of joy sound first, and sound so clearly that it will reverberate still through more sombre notes that must subsequently be sounded.

More has been written recently on the parables than on any other part of the New Testament. Suffice it is to say here that parable was characteristic of Jesus, though by no means invented by him, and that it was his rather poetic way of invoking in his hearers the new experience of the rule of God. The parable does not present the hearer with an abstract analysis or an illustration of a point of view, which can be considered later at leisure. It evokes emotional involvement and immediate response. At times, human nature being what it is, the spontaneous response is to take offence, and the possibility that those who experience the rule of God may suffer violence emerges in yet another form. But the parables are many and varied, and the simplest of them can evoke a quite complex response. Since they are ancillary to Jesus' action there is no need to categorize them—though I must confess that I tend to favour Matthew's sequence of beginning with the parable of the sower and ending with parables of wedding feasts and bridegrooms and entering into the joy of the Lord. It is so suggestive of the acted parable of the meal: the seed 'dying' buried in the dark earth, germinating, the oldest symbol of hope; the wheat put to the sickle in the joy of harvest time; and the final fellowship of the banquet.

But to begin with the note of joy: consider the tiny parables of the treasure hidden in the field we daily tramp across, the pearl hidden amongst the bric-a-brac of the pawnshops of our lives, the sudden joy of the discovery, and the people who sacrifice all they have, and do so joyfully, for the treasure which was there all along. The complex of emotions is clearly reminiscent of the meal, where we are asked to take as a precious gift what is already there for us, and in the gratitude of joy that is then felt to give it all again. And the openness of the table, the sheer indiscriminacy of the invitation to grace, is repeated in parable again and again. Publicans and sinners duly make their appearance: the publican is right before God rather than the Pharisee. The prodigal son commits a series of sins any one of which would to a Jew make him as one of the Gentiles, yet before he can finish his little formula of repentance and without a formal word of forgiveness yet spoken, the fatted calf is killed and the glad feast is under way. The old lags who did least work get every man a penny, as much as those who had borne the heat of the day; and it is the hated Samaritan who does the decent thing while the priests pass by. The wretches from the highways and byways take the place of the chosen ones at the new banquet of the kingdom of God. All this, of course, is highly offensive to those who have already decided upon the criteria that qualify people for God's grace. And since these parables simply reinforce even more indiscriminate praxis, the followers of this way may expect persecution, in addition to the sacrifice which the way in any case requires of them. Well may they ask not to be led into the trial, but to be delivered from the evil to come.

The cost of discipleship is clearly conveyed in stories about the fate of kings who go to war with half an army and the fate of men who set about building towers with insufficient resources. If you cannot rise to the joy of the kingdom, you are better to grovel along in your usual manner. But decision must not be delayed. The unjust steward was certainly unjust, but he knew what had to be done and he did it. Thus is the impression reinforced that the essence of the kingdom of God lies in actively relating to things as precious, as gift or grace already there, and not in some doctrine or theory, some message to be analysed carefully before measuring the assent that can reasonably be given to it. A gift is not a gift until it can be received with gratitude. A treasure is of value only to those who show their appreciation of it; for others it is another piece of bric-a-brac, a part of the field. And the test of whether one receives as gift and appreciates as treasure what is already there is one's ability to give again. There is dire warning in the story of the servant who receives mercy but refuses it to a fellow-servant.

### Jesus' relations of grace

An ordinary man at ordinary meals, but willing to break the ordinary sacramental bread with outcasts and sinners, relieving the common needs and ailments and praying for what was already there, and telling short complex stories about common characters and events in order to evoke some understanding of what he was already doing. Is there a brief way of summing up this reign of God which he took himself to be inaugurating? I have already suggested a phrase as pithy as Marx's 'relations of production' and quite similar to it: relations of grace.

Marx's relations of production consisted of a kind of praxis which, if it produced commodities, rendered all relations between persons, between persons and their work and between persons and nature, impersonal and destructive; but if it produced 'creative property' rather than private property, the same praxis could heal all relationships and enhance human life for all. But it can easily occur to the reader of Marx that a praxis which begins at the level of labour, however creatively and comprehensively this is understood, may already have missed a deeper level at which human relations to persons and to things are already distorted or in process of healing. This is the deeper level at which I relate to the finiteness of persons and things and to their common fragility, in short, the level at which I relate to ever-threatening nothingness, to 'unresting' death. And already at this level there is a choice of praxis: the praxis of clinging to people and things as finite as I am, in order to sustain my life in the face of existential anguish, but succeeding only in increasing desperation and fear, grasping and closing and making a fist. Or there is the praxis of holding as grace in the open, chaliced hands the riches of life, and transmitting life to all I meet. The latter, the praxis of Jesus, constitutes relations of grace, which must lie deeper within all relations of production, if the latter are ever to be experienced as salvific rather than demonic. For I cannot get to the point where my relationship with my product, my labour, others, nature, is co-creative of a better world, unless I can already relate to things and people as gifts or graces—my existential anguish would turn my product into a private possession, and it would do the same to you and to as many of your products as I could persuade you to part with, so that I could cling to them for security. Furthermore, if one begins with praxis at the level of relations of production one can easily see the whole cosmic project as a human achievement; but if one goes deeper to the level of grasping or of grace one is already either dicing with death in a game one must lose or beginning to be capable of letting go into a fathomless source all that one has and is and thus experiencing the source itself as the ultimate grace. At this deeper level one experiences either the divine or the demonic, in either case a power that is quite beyond all possibility of manipulation by the most benign forms of human production.

So Jesus in his activity evoked what can be called relations of grace. These do not exclude relations of production—Marx's analysis was quite right as far as it went—but they lie deeper within them, where they form a contrast with what can only be called relations of grasping; grasping at finiteness to sustain oneself, as Kierkegaard put it. Further, given the sheer ordinariness of the man Jesus, and the ordinary and hence universal symbolism of his meals, I cannot see that the relations of grace he evoked were more restricted than Marx's relations of production. Just as the latter affected all things and all people in all their activities, so relations of grace were not confined to contact with particular times or places. Nor was any sector of human behaviour, such as politics, outside Jesus' relations of grace, any more than Marx's relations of production.

Relations of grace, even more than relations of production, are inherently bound up with action, behaviour, living. It is only when someone who knows the power of the symbolism, and follows it through in practice, offers the symbolic gift of bread to me that I experience anything in life as grace, that the eye of my imagination can be opened to the gift character of all my life and of all that comes into it, and the power of grace can then transform my own intrinsically selfish existence. Without this originating experience of grace in act, the world of things and of people can easily seem at best an indifferent terrain to be plundered in my insatiable desire for existence, at worst a hostile place ever emphasizing and threatening my contingency. In the key activities of Jesus' public life people felt a benign and creative presence, a power that was pure grace, and this they were invited to call Abba, God. Or else they saw a devastating threat to the human barriers they had erected, at once their protection and their prison, and to the property lines they had drawn, all in the name of a rather different God, and they felt that the power and the presence encountered in Jesus were demonic. And in a vain attempt to put an end to that spirit in the world, they put him to death. It was a vain attempt indeed, because the power of this particuar kind of loving, the spirit that gives out of its profound sense of unrestricted grace, finds its most powerful expression in dying. By dying, as Jesus insisted, it lives. Therefore it is divine power, and those who receive it and live by it have already conquered death.

## Jesus and the other versions of the reign of God

The rival interpretations of God's kingdom, power, and glory with which Jesus came in conflict were, first, that of the Scribes and Pharisees and, in the end, that of the Temple priesthood itself and the Sadducee party. Jesus basically rejected the belief of the Pharisees (of all religions) that one can construct a set of rules by which the purity of a holy priesthood can be extended into the world, and with it God's rule. On the contrary, God's gracious reign is already in the world, his grace in the wheatfield and the vineyard, his forgiveness of all in the bread and wine, and anyone can extend that grace to anyone else. The Temple (Church) can celebrate this intimate and accessible presence, but it cannot bring it about. Paul, the converted Pharisee, was thus correct in saying that we are not under the law, but under grace. But Paul remained a Pharisee according to his own account of himself, presumably because he did not wish to condone antinomianism, much less immorality. People would always work out codes in order to regulate as best they could their relationships of grace, but the codes must now embody the universal relationships of grace and yield to these wherever necessary (the Sabbath was made for man). They would not be amongst the prerogatives of any particular group, to be extended thereafter to others.

The fact that Jesus in the end came into conflict with the Sadducee party, to which the Temple priesthood belonged, has often seemed to support those who insist that the cause of Jesus was religious and not political, that he was executed for religious and not for political reasons, and that the political figure of Pilate was involved only because he was bullied by priests whom he was too weak to resist. We cannot pause at this point in order to comment at any length on the (political?) motives of those who propose such clear-cut distinctions between religion and politics —except perhaps to say that churches which have confined themselves to 'spiritual' matters in states which have dealt out injustice to citizens or to strangers have done their fair share of political damage, and that those who are still unconvinced of this should read Marx *On the Jewish Question*.

As far as Jesus is concerned, the ordinariness of the man prevents any confinement of himself or his cause to the ranks of professional holy people, and the symbolism of his ordinary meals must be similarly unconfined: the relations of grace which he evoked and activated effect *all* human relationships in every human *polis*. Furthermore, the Sadducees clearly saw Jesus as one so close to the Fourth Philosophy that they feared specifically his 'sowing the seed of civil strife'—'if we let him alone, the Romans will come and will destroy our place and nation'; 'it is expedient that one man die for the people that the whole nation might not perish' (John 11: 48–50)—and Pilate explicitly executed Jesus between two Zealots as a messianic pretender.

So there is ample evidence to suggest that members of the Sadducee party, far from concurring in the view that Jesus was a religious agent to the exclusion of political involvement, saw in his cause and therefore in his person the probable sources of political upheaval. Far from confining themselves to religious reasons in this opposition to Jesus, and then having to trump up political reasons in order to bully a weak Pilate into an insupportable judicial decree, the Sadducees identify just those motives for bringing about the death of Jesus which could be considered to be closest to Pilate's own heart. The conduct of Jesus' cause as they saw it was threatening the rule of law and order as they understood it. The delicately balanced structures of puppet government and imperial powers, indeed the common understanding of political authority—common to Jewish priest and Roman governor alike—were therefore under threat. If we can know, then, why the Sadducees opposed Jesus and some wanted him dead, we shall also know why Pilate agreed to have him executed. Indeed we may already begin to suspect that this much advertised weakness of Pilate was not really the uncomplicated weakness of a spineless character, but the far more significant weakness of a man whose position of political authority depends upon the use of force and fear, and who cannot himself accept, though he may well be made to imagine, that leadership in human society could be exercised in any other way.

The relations of grace which Jesus inaugurated most certainly affected that texture of relationships between rulers and ruled which constitutes the political structures of human society. If we can discover, then, what practice distinguished Jesus' versions of the reign of God from that of the Sadducees we shall inevitably discover something about the essential Christian critique of all political power; we may learn something, too, of the age-old

Christian betrayal whereby, like the Sadducees of old, Christian leaders themselves imitate their secular counterparts, the descendants of Pilate. And we may well learn what distinguished Jesus from *all* rival versions of the reign of God at his time—indeed from all known forms of political leadership, in that they all had this at least in common, that they were ultimately prepared to resort to arms in order to defend their options for living. It is highly significant that both Sadducees and Pilate treated Jesus as the equivalent of a violent revolutionary—remember the reasons for his death which the Sadducees gave, and remember that Pilate executed Jesus as a messianic pretender between two violent Zealots. That is some measure of the sheer incomprehension of people of all religio-political persuasions who cannot see any means of getting their way other than through physical force, if only in the last resort. Or, perhaps, incomprehension is not quite the correct word. For Pilate and the Sadducees probably saw clearly enough what Jesus was proposing but, like all their imitators to this day, were terrified at the prospect of losing the only kind of authority they could understand. Then, like all frightened people do, they painted their opponent with their own brush, as a man who would bring violence, and in self-fulfilment of their own prophecy they used violence against him. No circle is more vicious than the circle of violence, and there is no logic of violence, however plausible it may sound, which is not in fact circular.

## Jesus' distinctive version of kingship

Well, then, like the Pharisees, Jesus brought the experience of God's rule to the people; unlike the Pharisees, and much to their offence, he invoked and activated this experience in the ordinariness of their lives rather than importing it from the Temple along with rules for priestly purity. Like the Sadducees, he clearly understood the reign of God to affect even political relationships; but what was it that made his experience of the reign of God different from that of the Sadducees in this respect and, in so far as politics always involve the recourse to arms, different from all other versions of the reign of God both then and now? The man without titles, the symbolism of his table-fellowship, and the relations of grace which he initiated, answer this question also. The short answer is that the lordship he experienced of God, and the only human lordship he could then allow, was lordship in the mode of slavery. And, as usual, the answer was given in act rather than words: I am among you as a slave. Relations of grace, in the mode which related leaders to all others, now cast the former in the role of servants to the latter; the gift of leadership above all consisted in breaking one's bread and pouring out one's cup for others.

But the answer is given more powerfully and more pointedly in a much neglected scene of the anointing of Jesus. The banquet which symbolized the reign of God was often called the messianic banquet; the age of God's final reign, the messianic age; its human agent, the Messiah. Messiah means 'anointed one', kings were anointed, and so the most natural form of expectation, which was shared by Jesus' closest followers, was that the Messiah would be a king. The gospels all have Jesus anointed. Jesus is king then? Of course. But as with any other title, the title does not define him or confine him to the terms of set expectations; he radically redefines the title and sets all human expectations on their heads. Matthew and Mark have Jesus anointed on the head at Bethany by a woman in the house of a leper; Luke has him anointed on the feet by a woman who is a sinner in the house of a Pharisee; John also has him anointed on the feet by Mary the sister of Lazarus—and it is specifically stated by Matthew and Luke, and less clearly by John, that he is anointed for his burial. Kings are anointed to ascend a throne. This king is anointed, two days before the fateful Passover, to ascend a cross, to be enthroned on Calvary, where women will follow their anointed leader. His crown is of thorns, his homage the mockery of soldiers, and his title, 'King of the Jews', is nailed like himself to his cross. When he is made to explain to Pilate that his kingship is not of this world (John 18: 36), we dare not, therefore, take this to mean that he is king in some separate spiritual realm, so that by the first separation of Church and State he becomes no threat to Caesar (and just as little use to him). No, Jesus' is a kind of kingship which revises totally all that this world has ever expected of kingship, and both priests and Pilate knew this very well; but none of them could accept it, so different was it from what they understood and exercised as power. I like D. M. McKinnon's suggestion that when some Jews asked Pilate to change the title on the cross, there was as much contempt in his voice for himself as for them in his answer: what I have written, I have written.

The parallel passage is the one in which Jesus lectures his disciples about their expectations of power and privilege: 'You know that the rulers of the Gentiles lord it over them, and their great ones exercise authority over them. It shall not be so among you; but whoever would be great among you must be your servant, and whoever would be first among you must be your slave' (Matt. 20: 25-7). Relations of grace could leave no set of human relationships untouched. The encounter with the true nature of divine power was equally at stake in all of them, including the relationship between leaders and subjects. The Sadducees might be no closer to a true understanding of the role of lordship which the true Father would condone than were the Pharisees.

## Jesus' rejection of the use of force

If the stories of the anointing of Jesus reveal the principal difference between Jesus' interpretation of the rule of God and that of the Sadducees, the story of Barabbas reveals the difference between Jesus and members of all four philosophies in the matter of the use of force. The Barabbas incident also occurs in all four gospels but it, too, gets little enough attention, and in the course of such attention as it does receive its significance is commonly lost in over-anxious efforts to decide upon historical detail. We must first notice that Barabbas bears the same title as Jesus, for this Aramaic name means Son of Abba, and Jesus, Son of God, called God 'Abba'. Barabbas is Jesus' doppelganger, but Barabbas is a Zealot, and the point of this story is to extend to all the choice that Pilate and the priest will make between the two sons of Abba. The truth of this story is that Pilate, priests and people will choose the Zealot and the god of war.

Picture the gospel scene in more detail. Two men are brought before Pilate, and for some reason which stories by their nature may but need not explain, he must execute only one of them. One is Barabbas, chained and furious, his short sword still stained with blood, his eyes leaving Pilate in no doubt that if he could, he would sink that same sword in Pilate's breast and die happily in the process. The other is Jesus, who would not crush a broken reed. Pilate need not hesitate. The crowds, prompted by their priests, can only tell him what he already knows he must do, however reluctantly. He must execute Jesus. He can let Barabbas go. Because Barabbas and he (and Caiaphas too) are brothers under the skin. They have exactly the same understanding of authority and how it is to be enforced, of power and how it is to be exercised. One small detail alone divides them: Pilate sits where Barabbas wants to sit. That is all. So Pilate can let Barabbas go, because Barabbas will never go far from him. He can always find Barabbas again, and find him again he will. He needs Barabbas, as Barabbas needs him (and the same is true, of course, for Caiaphas). Barabbas is the reason for his power, his prestige and his privileges; and in the mad, violent game of musical chairs that they play, he will provide just as good a reason for Barabbas.

But Jesus, who would die rather than kill, who proposes the leadership model of a slave . . . he would strip these officers of church and state of everything they take to be power, for the sake of unconditional grace, the love even of enemies, the utter generosity of the God he too calls 'Abba'. As a slave he has lived; as a slave, then, he must die. Crucifixion is the form of execution for slaves. The crowds cannot see this other kind of power either, this alternative way, the power of giving, of grace, the power, as Paul put it, made perfect in weakness. So crucify him. Release Barabbas. Barabbas is one of us. The crowds and their priests are no better than Pilate, and if in the story they seem worse, it is because Pilate shows some sense of the weakness of the only power which, as a friend of Caesar, he feels able to exercise. The moral of this story for Christians who make use of force and fear has seldom been drawn: Jesus has even less to do with those who wage war, in God's name or with God's supposed moral sanction, than he has to do with the other beliefs of Pharisee or Sadducee, Qumran convenanter or Zealot.

Fidelity to the reign of the God he called Abba, to the power that enabled one to die rather than betray it, to the glory that tabernacles only in grace, required from Jesus the ultimate self-emptying. For this all his meals prepared, and the Last Supper explicitly signified it. This the last petition of the Lord's Prayer anticipated. The spirit or power which he embodied as he initiated the relations of grace found its definitive form, its fullest outpouring, on the cross. For those who could take it, encounter with *that* spirit was encounter with God; in Jesus they could point to the presence of ultimate power. On the cross they saw him raised, exalted to lordship, breathing out the divine spirit to a dying world; Jesus himself, as Paul put it, now—now and not later—was a life-giving spirit. Here is the fountainhead of the Christian theology of the divinity of Jesus and of the crucified God.

\*    \*    \*

It seems hardly necessary to say that the whole life and teaching of Jesus was an act of thoroughly Jewish imagination, the living out of a totally Jewish faith, nourished in all its parts by the same long, rich, and varied religious tradition on which he, like rival interpreters of the rule of God, had been reared. There is therefore no Old Testament in the sense in which Christians have too often used that phrase, in the sense of a covenant abrogated by a newer one, much as one's last will abrogates any previous wills one might have made. Like the term Father as a title for God, the theme of covenant is of quite restricted relevance in what Christians call the Old Testament. Hence where the language of a new covenant is used by Jesus and his followers, this cannot be taken to mean that the Jewish faith has been superseded by another faith, that the Jewish faith had the sole and simple function of predicting the coming of this particular Christ. On the contrary, in the case of the new Jesus covenant, as in the cases of previous covenants, what is at issue is a radical reformulation, and, in the minds of those who do the reformulating, a purifying and revitalizing of the same original faith. Jesus, both in his own eyes and in the eyes of the more clear-sighted of his followers, is the fulfilment of the faith of Israel. His is the faith of Israel in its final and perfect form.

It seems hardly necessary to say this, in view of all that has gone before. But it may be useful nevertheless, for three reasons. First, in order to discredit further, if need be, the horrible history of Christian anti-Semitism. Second, in order to prepare the way for further developments in christology that would facilitate a dialogue between Jews and Christians, so that they might be able to see themselves as peoples who shared the same original faith, even if they still chose different versions of it. Third, and consequently so that Christians might be once and for all robbed of the ease with which they identify all those things of which Jesus was critical as specifically Jewish things, and so that attention to specks in Jewish eyes might no longer prevent them noticing the very similar-shaped motes in their own. For if Christianity and Judaism share the same basic original faith, then it is not altogether unlikely that the aspects of that faith which Jesus rejected in favour of his own version are still as much present in Christianity as in Judaism. Jews and Christians might well be more justified historically in uniting either for or against some of these aspects, or at least against their more questionable manifestations—the presumptions of a priestly caste, the legalism of a diseased zeal for God's law, religious exclusiveness and withdrawal symptoms from the world, unhealthy territorial interests and a preference for force and fear—than they ever could be in staying apart because of the tragic accident of an early break between them. Many Christians, like many Jews, undoubtedly prefer other versions of the reign of God to the one for which Jesus died; to that extent they stand alike before the challenge of Jesus. But Jesus and his challenge, as a man of Jewish faith is as accessible to the historian as any other man who shaped a tradition and by doing so changed the shape of history.

What was perhaps most radical about Jesus was the way in which his personal act of historical imagination tended to cancel the distinction between the sacred and the profane. Most people committed to religion, Jews and Christians included, find that feature of his cause most difficult to accept. But it is an unavoidable feature of his mission; indeed it is the distinctive way in which he secured the future of those universalist themes which had surfaced elsewhere in Israel's traditions. The cancellation of the distinction between the sacred and the profane was not achieved, it must already be clear, by the extension of the rules governing sacred people and times and places to the rest of the world. On the contrary, the presence of divine spirit was to be encountered in the commonest of things and events, in the most ordinary joys and tragedies of life. That is why it must be insisted that the meals in which the encounter took place with the power made perfect in weakness were ordinary meals, and the man who made the encounter possible an ordinary man. This does not imply that there must be no special meals specifically named Eucharists. It may seem paradoxical, but it does seem obvious nevertheless, that it takes a special meal to evoke the most profound existential, indeed religious, symbolism of all meals, and the universal relevance of that symbolism for, to take some examples, the feeding of the hungry of the world and the extension of friendship to enemies—though it must be added that the special meals can succeed in their special sacramental roles only if that radical and fundamental symbolism of all meals is made real in act. The particular is the door to the universal in which the encounter with the divine is possible.

Something similar must be said about the ordinary man. Jesus could not have the universal significance his followers claim for him, as the one in whose powerful presence the very spirit of God can be encountered, if he is to be restricted to any category, class or caste, for then the presence of God could be encountered only where such a category or class of men was operative. They have not felt the full force of the Christian doctrine of incarnation who do not realize that Jesus was a man, just a man, but a man for a' that.

# 5

# The Body of Christ

Both writer and reader might have followed the argument of the book up to this point—the former in the sense in which arguments in systematic theology, like plots and characters for novelists, begin to take on a life of their own; the latter more dispassionately and with less commitment to any final assent— only to find themselves at this point brought up sharply by the sudden realization of how very historical, how thoroughly bodily, indeed, how utterly pictorial, all talk of God has by now become. An unknown Jew heaving desperately after his last few suffocating breaths on a Roman cross . . . *this* is divine spirit inspiring a spiritless world? This broken body is breathing divine life into a dying world? Well, yes, if crucifixion is resurrection, as at least for Mark and John it certainly is; and if resurrection is equivalent to divine lordship, as in the New Testament in general it certainly is. Yes, of course, only because those strangled breaths and that writhing body belong to this faithful man, whose fidelity unto this death was a greater thing than any law.

And so this is divine spirit incarnate. This, and not the obscure birth in a legendary manger, is the fullest incarnation of divine spirit; this is the body so much and so essentially instrument of spirit that its very disintegration at death lets that spirit loose in the world. Of this body especially it can be said that never did it breathe this spirit more fully than when it breathed its last, breathed it out in final self-emptying disintegration. Never was this body more spiritual than when it allowed itself to be broken in utter faithfulness to the grace which is at the heart of all things. That is why resurrection, which occurred on Calvary, is symbolized equally well by raising-up and by spirit-breathing imagery.

But what of the spirit of Jesus now that that body is gone? *Where* the body has gone is of no concern to us here, for what we want to know about is the spirit of Jesus in this world. We are as yet quite unconcerned about any world other than this, the only one we know, and so it does not matter *for purposes of answering this question* whether the body of Jesus has now disintegrated in some grave or has been taken off to some other place. In either case it is no longer here. Our pressing question still is: does the spirit which enlivened Jesus' body to breaking point—the spirit which some thought to be Beelzebub and others believed to be the divine spirit—now breathe bodiless in this world, assuming of course that it does still breathe in this world?

The whole argument of this book would surely press for a negative answer to that question. Not just the argument that spirit is opposed to flesh in scriptural terms, and not to body; that a person's body or a body of persons, in everything they have and do, can be either flesh or spirit. Nor just the argument of the chapter which sought to bring together for mutual illumination the themes of divinity, resurrection, and Eucharist—though this is the central argument which must press for a negative answer to the question, and it will bear some summary repetition here. But the whole argument about history and imagination and praxis with which the book began, and which makes us look to time and the concrete particular in order to see the universal and the eternal.

According to the narrative sequence adopted by Luke/Acts, the spirit which came upon Jesus at birth and baptism (and which Jesus breathed consummately in his death) came from Jesus upon the body of his followers and was embodied thenceforth in their being and doing. John's 'other paraclete' passages, when taken in context, can be read without strain as saying that the disciples who form the Johannine community now have the spirit which is to them and to their time what Jesus was to their predecessors in his time. But the greatest New Testament theologian of the spirit is Paul: it is he who brings us the fullest scriptural assurance that divine spirit is as embodied after Jesus' death as it was during and before that epochal event; it is he who leads us to the master symbol in this area of discourse, the symbol of the body of Christ—and symbols, of course, are ways of knowing the depth of reality.

The full impact of Paul's theology can be felt only by those who realize that for Paul the risen Jesus *is* a divine or, as he himself says, a life-giving spirit. As J. D. G. Dunn put it towards the end of a more general analysis of *Jesus and the Spirit*, resurrection meant that Jesus became 'that Spirit which believers experience as the source and power of their new life and new relationship with God'. And he goes on to issue two rather striking statements: 'if Christ is now experienced as Spirit, Spirit is now experienced as Christ', and 'as the Spirit was the "divinity" of Jesus, so Jesus became the personality of the Spirit'.[1] Jesus now *is* spirit, and for those who can take it, divine and not demonic spirit; but not disembodied spirit. In Paul's own use of the symbol, the body of Christ, in the key chapter 12 of 1 Corinthians, it is clear that the followers of Jesus are the body of Christ precisely because it is the spirit/Christ who animates them corporally and not—to take another, but clearly inept explanation—because Jesus is the head and they are all arms and legs and so on, and a distinct Holy Spirit, distinct both from the raised Jesus and from them, animates the lot of them. Jesus is Risen/ Lord or spirit and, incarnate as ever, is bodied forth in the rag, tag, and bobtail that followed him. It is a small step to say that this bodying forth in the world takes place *par excellence* when this motley crew breaks very bodily bread and shares a cup of wine; and that small step, it has been suggested already, is fully justified by the ancient theology of calling down the spirit to make the body of Christ really present, to make it 'appear' in the world.

There is nothing new in this. Resurrection, lordship, being spirit—all are ways of claiming what later came to be called, more abstractly, the divinity of Jesus; all are ways of claiming the incarnation of God. If there is anything new, it is no more than a new emphasis, an emphasis upon the continuity of incarnation. Divine spirit, experienced by his followers as the spirit that was and is Jesus, is as incarnate in the world today as it was in ancient Galilee. It is now fully incarnate, in what is known after Paul as the body of Christ. And just as divine spirit was vulnerable to flesh in the body of Jesus, as his temptations quite clearly illustrate, so it has been vulnerable since to all that is flesh in the body of Christ that is the church. Many who have encountered the church down the centuries have thus encountered flesh rather than spirit, demonic spirit rather than divine spirit, darker death rather than risen life.

The implications of this line of thought are many and varied, but only the following may be selected for a short chapter in this short book: first, a theological implication, that the church, the body of Christ, is the third 'persona' of the Christian Trinity, as Jesus of Nazareth is the second 'persona'; second, a practical implication, that the true church is found only where the spirit of Jesus fashions bodily life and death like his. This is not a doctrine of an 'invisible church', for spirit works in this world always as body (as every sensible Stoic knew); but it does relegate to matters of incidental interest those intense modern ecumenical pursuits of agreement on matters of church order, authority, and ministry.

## The Christian experience of God as Trinity

People cannot encounter a power in this world and name it God without thereby forming some image or concept of what divinity is like 'in itself'. The followers of Jesus, having reflected long and carefully, finally conceived of God as triune, three 'personae' in one divine being, though to this day they continue to argue vociferously amongst themselves as to what precisely such terms might be taken to mean. Amongst the specific problems about which they argued were these two. First, was there, even before the conception of Jesus (sometimes referred to as *the* incarnation), a disembodied person in something like the human sense of the word 'person', and if so, how was this person thought to be God without multiplying divinities, and how was he (?) related to Jesus of Nazareth, a human person like the rest of us? Second, was there really a disembodied spirit who was divine and yet distinct from the God Jesus called Father and from the 'other' divine person who pre-existed Jesus, and if so, how was this known, and how was it that divinities were not yet further multiplied?

It would not be right to rehearse here the history of Trinitarian theology. Libraries have been written on the subject. But a suggestion might be made, the simplicity of which should not tempt us to dismiss it too quickly. It is this: the trouble which lies at the root of the two major problems outlined above surely concerns the disembodied, the discarnate, status of the second and third personae. For whether we take as our starting point the Christian experience of a distinctive power erupting in the world, or the normative Christian Scriptures, all that we ever seem to encounter, all we ever seem to have described for us under the terms 'son' and 'spirit' is, in the case of the former at least, a very incarnate figure indeed. And in the case of the spirit, as far as the Bible is concerned, it always seems to refer either to God *simpliciter*, or to the 'divinity' embodied in Jesus, or to the 'risen' Jesus who is, of course, now embodied in the body of Christ.

Karl Barth has been the strongest proponent of the view that if we use pre-existence language of the Son of God, as indeed we must if we want to say that divinity in itself (in 'eternity') is characterized by what it freely effected through Jesus, then we must say that Jesus of Nazareth, the individual man of flesh and blood, and with this life-history and no other, 'pre-existed' in God's very being. We have no authority from Scripture, Barth insists, and none, naturally, from any other source, which could enable us to say anything at all about a discarnate 'Son' or 'Word' of God.

This material from *Church Dogmatics*, ii. 2 fits quite well in actual fact with Barth's theology of the Trinity with which he begins that magisterial work. For those who have struggled through that long and subtle analysis of Christian Trinitarian thought will realize at the end that they have been told very little: only that God's revelation in Jesus of Nazareth and the ensuing spirit that makes us its receptive embodiment allow us to believe that all this involved some self-differentiation in the divinity itself, and that we are given some scriptural terms in which to talk of that divine self-differentiation, but that such terminology does not allow us to understand it in the least. We are then left with Jesus of Nazareth as the second persona of the Trinity and have nothing to say about any other second persona, other than the persona who was and is Jesus of Nazareth.

A similar logic applies to spirit, with the slightly confusing addition that spirit can name divinity itself in abstraction, one might say, from its self-differentiation in the mode of Jesus of

Nazareth. But it can also, as we noted, name Jesus of Nazareth as the incarnate divine power erupting in the world on Calvary. So, if we wish to use the word spirit, as very ancient church traditions allow us to use it, for yet another persona of God, we shall either have to revert to talk of a discarnate Holy Spirit and land ourselves in similar problems to those that cripple all discourse on a discarnate Son, or we shall have to follow to its conclusion the logic of previous chapters and point to an embodied divine spirit, the body of Christ, as the third persona of God.

So, then, the only divine Trinity we know is composed of the power made present as Jesus of Nazareth in his present body which is the church. In other words, for followers of Jesus, the personal God is encountered in the person of Jesus of Nazareth and the person of Jesus of Nazareth is encountered in the church. Three personae in one divine being-in-act; not to be imagined as different 'dramatis personae' who dominate different and successive acts in the history of being. Rather does the veiled person of God emerge as the person of Jesus through the corporate personality of the church. Behind this dynamic presentation there may well be an inner self-differentiation of divinity, but we cannot know and therefore cannot talk about that. What we do believe is that divine spirit is the spirit encountered in Eucharist, the spirit which is Jesus, and on that faith, in that spirit, if we follow Jesus, we risk everything with quite astonishing grace. The difficulty in believing that the church is divine is of the same order as the difficulty in believing that Jesus is divine—though it is increased by the blatant infidelities of the church in all ages. These infidelities also enhance one's impression of the vulnerability of God, vulnerable because permanently incarnate, vulnerable now in an unfaithful body, really now taking both sin and suffering unto himself in the hope that indomitable grace will be victorious.

## The dismembered body

In the long and often acrid history of the debate about the true church of Jesus the Christ one fact at least has been obvious to everyone: that not all who claim to belong to Christ's church, or who on some criteria can be described as members of it, are good people. Furthermore, at a time when it is fashionable to talk of evil being endemic to institutions as such, it is the institutions which Christians have evolved over the course of time that are seen as the prime agents of Christian betrayal. The very phrase 'the church' most commonly denotes the offices and their incumbents who act towards the mass of members or on their behalf. So complaints about 'the church' can usually be taken to refer to official acts, thus implicitly exonerating 'the faithful'. On the other side of the coin, when people think about redeeming the more obvious failures of the church—when they think, for instance, of healing the debilitating divisions within the Christian movement itself—they look to institutional change as the most essential, the change without which no other change can make any progress at all. Thus are 'the faithful' as free of the responsibility to make things better as they seem free of guilt for all that is worst. A fair enough deal, one might think, for both pastors and people. The people have no onerous responsibility, but neither do they bear the corresponding burden of guilt; the pastors take the blame, but then they also have the authority, the power, and the position, or whatever small measure of these may be left to ecclesiastics in the modern world.

So it comes about that the commonest strategy when faced with the historical failures of Christianity is either to claim that an invisible church, known presumably to God, is the true church, or to clamour for institutional action. It is the argument of this section that the former option is false because it propagates a false dichotomy between spirit and body, because there is in fact no real presence of the spirit of Christ in this world which is not detectable in bodily form; and that the latter option is equally false when, in search of truth, it looks first to institutions and offices. These, as far as our records reveal, did not feature in the mind of the founder at all; their constitutional form was entirely optional to the early followers of Jesus (though tradition has since lent legitimacy to most of them), and it is only the spirit in which they too are 'bodied forth' by their incumbents which is of interest to the Christian faith.

I begin with the institutions of the Roman Catholic Church.

I do so because it is to these that I owe my own critical loyalty, and I am therefore most familiar with their forms and operation. But the offices and institutions of other churches are very similar. Eastern Orthodox and Anglicans differ mainly in their views of the See of Rome—though that is currently under negotiation—and so much that is said in the following pages must apply equally to them. In fact many of the churches of the Reformation are more clerical than they would wish us to believe. Although their theory does not propose such a clear-cut distinction between officers and others as more hierarchical churches, their practice may in fact provide points of contact with much that must now be said.

The most recent of the most authoritative documents of the Roman Catholic Church, the documents of Vatican II, expressly adopted from Vatican I (1870) 'all this teaching about the institution, the perpetuity, the force and reason for the sacred primacy of the Roman Pontiff'.[2] Vatican I had decreed that 'the primacy of jurisdiction' was immediately and directly given to Peter by Christ. In addition—although this second point seems to be more of an inference from the church's permanent need for a rock than yet another piece of selective and idiosyncratic exegesis —whosoever succeeds Peter in this See of Rome 'which was founded by him' enjoys 'by the same institution' the same primacy of jurisdiction. Jurisdiction is a word which needs some definition, and we shall probably not go far wrong if we adopt that offered by the Anglican–Roman Catholic International Commission's *Final Report*: the authority or power necessary for the effective fulfilment of an office. We are therefore very much in the presence of the offices of an institution, and of their legislative, judicial, and coercive powers. Their alleged powers of coercion may now be thought more 'spiritual' than temporal—exclusion from the sphere of God's grace rather than burning at the stake—but they need be thought none the less real for that.

Vatican II then goes on to deal with the other apostles. These apostles, it declares, Jesus fashioned into a 'fixed group' like a college, over which he placed Peter. These apostles in turn 'took care to appoint successors in this hierarchically structured society', and they 'authorised the arrangement that, when these men

should have died, other approved men would take up their ministry'. This sequence of authorized events allows Vatican II to
conclude that the bishops of the church down the centuries have
'by divine institution' succeeded to the place of the apostles, as
popes have succeeded to Peter's place, and with similar jurisdiction, except that only Peter's jurisdiction is 'supreme'.

This jurisdiction is then said to be valid in three conjoined
areas—sanctifying, teaching, and governing. The first means that
the 'sacred power' of priestly orders belongs by Christ's institution to Peter and the eleven and their successors; the second that
they are the 'authentic' teachers of orthodox doctrine and interpreters of the Scriptures; the third that they are the 'officers of
good order' in the Christian community, the guardians, as we
might say in more contemporary jargon, of law and order. All
this is contained in Chapter III of Vatican II's Constitution 'On
The Church'; and it is all, of course, a foundation myth.

This does not simply mean that it is untrue, for myths are as
capable of telling the truth as are more literal compositions—in
areas of human experience which plumb its very depths they can
indeed be quite superior ways of exploring the truth. The truth of
this myth lies in the fact that this major Christian group has over
long periods of time adopted this manner of meeting the essential
historical need to organize itself in order to preserve and promul-
gate the riches it has received from Jesus, and that it believes that
this manner of organization is in line with much that Jesus and his
earliest followers are said to have done. But one need only engage
in Gadamer's fusion of horizons—that is to say, one need only
read the Scriptures and other early church documents with this
constitutional law in mind—in order to begin to see that neither
Jesus nor his earliest followers can be literally credited with it,
and that very different styles of church constitution are just as
much in line with what they are said to have done.

## The Twelve

The history behind 'the Twelve' would take a book on its own to
investigate. During the recent Gunning Victoria Jubilee Lectures
at Edinburgh James Charlesworth explained why he had now
ceased to hold the view held by so many New Testament experts

that the early Christians invented the choice of twelve by Jesus, as part of their claim to be the new Israel because Jesus was the true Messiah of God. Despite the fact that the names of the Twelve differ in the accounts given (Mark 3: 13–19; Matt. 10: 1–4; Luke 6: 12–16; Acts 1: 13), and that there are 'rival' groupings in the tradition—sometimes select groups (Peter, James, and John, and at times Andrew; Peter and John in Acts); sometimes larger numbers referred to simply as 'the disciples', or the seventy or seventy-two to whom documents in the New Testament record Jesus gave such tasks as binding and loosing, preaching, forgiving sins, and so on, which elsewhere he gives to one or to a more select group—Charlesworth now joins those who believe that Jesus himself probably did choose twelve. The intent, however, could be the same whether we are dealing with an act of Jesus or an early Christain invention: not to set up an institution for church government, but to symbolize that Jesus through his disciples was indeed renewing Israel, issuing in the reign of God, the messianic age. The implication of Charlesworth's move, and of others who agree with him, is then to push that intent, with due regard for the probabilities of history, back to the life of the historical Jesus. But this is a very long way from the literal terms of our foundation myth. The picture of the Twelve busily appointing their own successors and arranging for these in turn to do likewise to the end of time is entirely a creation of the foundation myth itself, though this foundation myth, in one form or another, is very old.

Mark and Matthew have Jesus sit down to the Last Supper with the Twelve (Luke has 'his apostles', and John says he sat down with his disciples), and we shall deal with the eucharistic implications for church leadership later. It is Luke, if the same Luke did write Acts, who gives the impression that the reconstituted Twelve (with the election of Matthias) formed some kind of fixed group in Jerusalem, at least for a time, and that they sometimes acted in concert, in dealing with the problem of the Hellenists, for instance (Acts 6: 2), and, *if* the phrase 'the apostles' can be taken as equivalent to 'the Twelve' at least in Luke's case, in sending Peter and John to Samaria (Acts 8: 14: here they would act with some authority towards Peter, 'sending' him on a mission!). But it is generally accepted that Luke's sense of history, such as it was, is very much at the service of his major theological preoccupations, and in particular of his own scheme of salvation history. Jerusalem with its dramatis personae, especially Peter and the eleven, is the centre from which the gospel goes out to other Jews and to Gentiles. So Luke has the risen Jesus appear and commission his apostles in Jerusalem, while Matthew has the commissioning of 'eleven' take place in Galilee, John has undifferentiated disciples commissioned, probably in Jerusalem, and the author of John 21 has a more restricted number, some of them members of the Twelve, meet Jesus for a commissioning scene at the Sea of Tiberias. Nothing much of genuine historical value can be gleaned from all of this about the activities of the Twelve after Jesus' death; in fact, apart from Peter, we know little or nothing about the other members of this symbolic group.

Luke notwithstanding, it is impossible to restrict the title 'apostles' in the New Testament to the Twelve. Paul, who on Luke's own account was as great a missionary preacher as Peter or any other, was in his own view as much an apostle as any and that by no man's commissioning. And on Luke's own showing also, James the brother of Jesus, who was not one of the Twelve, could be as authoritative in Jerusalem as any of them. No; the historical origin of church offices and institutions and of the kind of jurisdiction which these finally claimed is a very different story from that told in the Roman Catholic foundation myth.

## The quest for the historical Peter

What, then, of Peter? The quest for the historical Peter is even more difficult than the quest for the historical Jesus. There are as many Peters in the New Testament as there are authors concerned with his career. He was a man named Simon or Simeon whom Jesus nicknamed Cephas ('rock' in Aramaic, *petros* in Greek). He appears to have made some sort of confession of Jesus during the latter's lifetime; he also seems to have quite seriously mistaken Jesus' purpose in the process. Nothing is more characteristic of the man than a kind of bumbling enthusiasm. He has been presented to posterity as the big fisherman, but we seafaring folk continue to be appalled by his penchant for jumping overboard and, of course, as one would expect, sinking like a rock (Good old Rocky! Gone overboard again!). What is most frequently lacking in interpretations of Jesus is the probability that he must have had a strong sense of humour. He *must* have had if he was to deal for one day with such characters as this. So he nicknamed this one Rocky, with great affection and unlikely hope. If Peter ever finally managed to see the point, his sheer ebullience would give him a commanding lead.

In any case, this tradition of his faulty confession, in addition no doubt to his role in the infant community of Jesus' followers, won for him the image of spokesperson amongst leaders and on this image some early portraits were elaborated. Luke in particular elaborates, if Luke did really write a Book of Acts so inferior to the gospel which now bears his name—though even with Luke it is impossible to conclude that Peter is a superior in some official sense to, say, James the brother of Jesus. No sense of 'supreme jurisdiction' comes across at any point.

It is obvious from reports of his journeying as well as from the variety of places in the New Testament in which his name was presumed to be known that Peter was no mean missionary. And it is a reliable inference from New Testament hints and from extrabiblical evidence that he finally reached Rome and indeed, like Paul, that he there bore the supreme testimony (martyrdom) which according to Jesus himself was required of the true Christian shepherd. But it is quite unlikely that he was ever a 'presbyter' in any settled Christian community, and as certain as such things can ever be that he was never 'Bishop of Rome' and as such the founder of that see, as the foundation myth describes him. He hands on no primacy of jurisdiction to anybody, either as head of a mythical college or in any other capacity. His figure is too human, too large, to be so circumscribed by the canon lawyers. He is far too important for the origins of Christianity and for our understanding of it to be the incumbent of any office which they have so far managed to describe.

Beyond that the New Testament portraits of Peter multiply to the point of offering us *un embarrass de richesse*. To Paul he was no doubt an authoritative source of tradition about Jesus, since he was a close and constant companion from the latter's baptism to his death, though the fact that this tradition was divine revelation to Paul was no more due to 'flesh and blood' in Paul's case than it was in Peter's (compare Gal. 1: 16 with Matt. 16: 17). Peter was, in addition, one of 'those who were of repute' in Jerusalem. But Peter's conduct in his table-fellowship at Antioch (Gal. 2: 11ff.) proved to Paul at least that he could still after all this time fail to see 'the truth of the Gospel', his very importance making it all the more necessary that he be once more reprimanded and his failure to understand once more brought to his notice.

Mark paints the darkest portrait of Peter, especially in 14: 71 where the suggestion is that Peter in denying Jesus actually cursed him, and in 8: 33 where Jesus calls Simon not Rock but Satan. But then Mark's is in many ways the bleakest of the accounts of Christianity in the New Testament, obsessed as it appears to be with the way in which the groups and persons closest to Jesus misunderstood, abandoned, and betrayed him. There are no consoling and consolidating appearances of the risen Jesus in Mark's account. The revelation of Jesus as God's Son takes place during his tragic life and death, and only those who take the way of the cross will ever witness to it. Mark knows of no offices or officers guaranteed in the truth. Some profess to see in the (undelivered) message of the women at the gospel's end a hint of Peter's rehabilitation, but it would take a very uninhibited visionary indeed to see a primacy of jurisdiction.

Matthew's substantial re-edition of Mark's confession scene (Matt. 16: 16–19) has offered the foundation myth its most frequently invoked text-proof. Though Matthew adds that Simon is a rock of stumbling for Jesus (16: 23—yet another, very different, use of the rock symbol), he also adds the symbolism of the keys of the kingdom and of the power of binding and loosing. This is, inevitably, a heavily disputed text. Much depends on whether the power of the keys is more extensive than that of binding and loosing, for the latter is elsewhere (18: 18) given to all the disciples (not just to the Twelve). The dispute looks likely to continue. It is unlikely that historical method will ever solve it, and for any one institution to claim the power to interpret it 'authentically' in its own favour would be just too obvious a form of self-approval.

Luke is kindest to Peter: he even takes the editorial liberty of omitting entirely Jesus' rebuke to Peter which his source contains—these inspired authors took extraordinary liberties with their inspired sources! But enough has been said about Luke. In John's account of the origin and nature of the Christian way Peter retains a certain prominence as spokesperson but he is not called first, and his confession of Jesus is given no particular notice. John alone recounts the washing of the feet incident in which Peter shows once again his by now familiar penchant for enthusiastic misunderstanding, and it is John who names Peter as the one who thought it best to fight their way out of Gethsemane. But the distinctive thrust of this gospel is surely to portray instead 'the disciple whom Jesus loved'—who was probably not even one of the Twelve—as the one whom Jesus favoured, the one who enjoyed a primacy in his love. Peter may well have been rehabilitated, as the added chapter 21 suggests, and may have died the Christian shepherd's death, but the 'disciple whom Jesus loved' *followed* him to the court of the High Priest and to the cross. He never fled and he never denied, and hence his authoritative witness is not one whit subordinate to that of Simon the Rock. That is the clear conviction of the authors of the Fourth Gospel.

## The early years of the Church

The historical origins of offices in the Christian community and of the jurisdiction which their incumbents came in time to claim are therefore much more difficult to describe than our foundation myth would ever lead one to suspect, and they have little enough to do with 'divine' institution through Jesus or his missionary companions. There is no need to attempt here such an elaborate task as the description of these origins, and indeed it would be impossible to do so. Clearly there was a time when acquaintances of Jesus were still alive amongst the growing number of his followers, or at least *their* first converts and companions. During this time the nascent communities of Christians, as they came to be called, were not without leaders, those 'who labour among you, lead you and admonish you'. In fact there appears to have been quite a variety of these: apostles and their 'fellow-workers', prophets, teachers, prominent householders, hold in common, 'the real presence', points to a common sense that Jesus is present in this sacrament as he is in no other activity of the Christian community. And if these churches all believe, as they appear to do, that it is the spirit of Jesus which reconciles the estranged, it would be strange if they then assumed that they should first negotiate their reunions—even if they attributed success in their negotiations to the spirit, as they usually do—and then carry their success into the 'real presence'. For what? To be endorsed? Or just expressed? A rather supernumerary role for the 'real presence', one might conclude.

and so on (but no priests, and no restriction either, apparently, of leadership roles to males), and relationships between these, where they existed at all, seem to have varied also. Though some institutional forms from surrounding Jewish/Gentile religious and secular life may already at this time have been in the process of adoption—the presbyterate, or the elders, the episcopacy of 'overseers'—no thought is yet given to institutional means of preserving the good news in its purity.

Naturally when these first apostles or apostolic men died, and all the usual dangerous symptoms from party loyalties to down-right villainy threatened the integrity of the new movement, some thought was given to regularizing matters by having settled and more centralized institutions with carefully described duties and prerogatives, with some description of how people should be appointed to office and of the kind of people who could expect to be appointed. Bishops, for instance, should be married men, according to 1 Timothy 3: 2.

I feel reasonably sure from all that I have read about it that the First Epistle of Peter is pseudonymous, that it makes good use of the obvious association of Peter's ultimate witness (*martyrdom*) with Rome and that, like *I Clement*, it seeks to extend Rome's influence over far-flung local churches, in particular those Pauline churches in Asia Minor which it mentions. In the amazingly rapid spread of the new Jesus-movement the political position of Rome made it the obvious destination of ambitious missionaries like Peter and Paul, and an equally obvious choice when at a later date the need was felt for settled and centralized institutions.

The Second Epistle to Timothy is written in the name of Paul, and a comparison of this with the Second Epistle of Peter is quite instructive. Both attempt to exercise a magisterium as it later came to be called, an authority in teaching which attempts to obviate false interpretations of the gospel. Both were very likely written from Rome and the latter, written in Peter's name, implies the authority to correct even some interpretations of Paul's difficult letters. A sign here, perhaps, that a magisterium beginning to be exercised in Peter's name is already outstripping one exercised in Paul's? In the *Didache*, a quite authoritative document of the early second century AD, we may actually catch a glimpse of the process by which an earlier leadership of 'prophets and teachers' begins to become institutionalized by the co-option of 'bishops and deacons'. And so it goes on. We have no manual of constitutional law from the church of the first century, nor could one have been written. We can but construct a patchy picture of an extremely varied development of very gradually institutionalized forms of leadership.

For the first century of the new movement's history, then, 'apostolicity' did not refer to any line of official appointees unbroken from the first apostles—for there was no such line—and thence to the things they taught. It referred rather to the gospel which the first apostles and their followers preached, celebrated liturgically and practised; and any Christian community which preserved the gospel was thereby apostolic, however it was organized or led. The rule of faith, as it came to be called, was thus handed on in a variety of forms.

One of these took the shape of a collection of writings which gradually came to be recognized as a canon of Scripture comparable to the emerging Jewish canon and *hence* seen to be divinely inspired. This was an apostolic collection—apostolicity was the criterion of its selection also—but in this connection it must be noted that one of the chief ways of maintaining apostolic succession in the earliest Christian community once the original apostles were dead was to write books or letters as if from them. This practice of pseudonymous authorship, so frowned upon in a different cultural climate, thus answered the problem of time's erosion of apostolic ranks. Hence a community which lived by these apostolic writings was apostolic or had the apostolic succession, for it lived by the faith which 'apostles or apostolic men' had first preached.

In the course of the second century AD the shape of community leadership became standardized, and the origin of institutions long since familiar to papal and episcopal churches begins to be seen. Over the succeeding centuries the nature and extent of the jurisdiction which now belongs to such institutions was laid down. It is neither necessary nor possible here to trace this long process of development. Enough has been said to explain how it can reasonably be held that several forms of church organization, in addition to papal and episcopal forms, are equally compatible with the acts and words of Jesus and of his earliest followers, and the fact that some of them developed (again?) relatively late in Christian history does not prove the slightest case against their validity or against the apostolicity of the gospel they preach, celebrate and live. It is a thoroughly Christian thing—and it may be the only Christian thing to do in this area of Christian existence—to offer full adult loyalty to one's own church ministry, as institutional leadership came to be called, while acknowledging the equal validity of the ministries of other Christian churches.

## The issue of 'sanctification'

But surely, one might think, though these conclusions might be acceptable for two of the areas of jurisdiction defined in the Roman Catholic foundation myth, the areas of teaching and of community discipline, they must be inadmissible in the area of what the myth calls sanctification. That is to say, though Jesus and his apostles made no institutional provision for a succession of official teachers and officers of good order, Jesus himself surely ordained those who could thereafter preside at the Lord's Supper and administer all ancillary means of sanctification, and *that* ordination at least must have come down in an unbroken line?

Here indeed is the heart of the matter, for that tame little sacristy word 'sanctification' in fact denotes the power of God unleashed to take up and heal a broken world, to make blessed or whole and happy all those who share the world's age-old misery, and to condemn to self-destruction those who ignore or oppose it. Correcting false interpretations, constructing orthodox doctrines, keeping order and imposing proper discipline: these, by contrast, are relatively harmless occupations and do not normally arouse passions greater than those involved in the rumblings of minor rebellion and ritual fits of scholarly pique. But in the area so quaintly called sanctification fear is easily evoked, and fear is the most destructive of emotions. Fear of ultimate power has been at the origin of every attempt to draw a line between the sacred and the profane, of every effort to confine the sacred power to set places and times and persons. So when the Constitution 'On the Church' from Vatican II insisted that there is a difference of essence and not just one of degree between the common priesthood of the faithful and the ministerial or hierarchical priesthood (par. 10), and when it declared that the latter alone are 'endowed with sacred power' (par. 18), the sentiments it expressed were not those of a power-hungry Christian clerical caste, for the percentage of powermongers amongst the Christian clergy is no greater than in any other class. The sentiments are older and they are ubiquitous. They can lead a great many people to insist that Jesus, too, should have harnessed the divine power to particular people and to the ritual times and places where such people officiate. That Jesus did not do so, that the nature of the power he identified as divine would positively prevent him from doing so, that is pehaps the most difficult lesson which the majority of his followers still have to learn.

## The central importance of the Christian community

Schillebeeckx in his later years has proved to be the true pioneer of contemporary Roman Catholic theology. His writings on ministry were primarily inspired by the need to liberate Roman Catholic theory and practice from the straitjacket to which Roman ecclesiastical law had long confined them, but the implications of his scholarship are of the greatest significance, not just for Roman Catholic revision of this part of its foundation myth, but for the proper reunion of divided Christendom to which the unrevised form of this myth threatens still to pose an insuperable obstacle.

There seems to be no gainsaying Schillebeeckx's conclusions that in the beginning it was the local community that celebrated or, as modern jargon would have it, concelebrated the Eucharist. Nobody had to be specially ordained to celebrate the Supper or to preside at it. No special 'sacred power' was conferred on anyone for the purpose. There were no priests in this new religion. Its founder was not a priest; the Letter to the Hebrews uses the symbol of the high priest to interpret his life, just as other writings had used other titles for this same purpose, but that is all. That is why the earliest Christian sources have no record whatever of any 'sacred power' to celebrate the Eucharist being conferred or handed on.

Naturally, since the Eucharist was *the* ritual action of the new communities, it was an organized affair. More than likely someone presided. And the presidency more than likely followed the varied and evolving patterns of community leadership in general. In the *Didache*, for example, there is clear evidence of presidency by teachers/prophets, to whose ranks in this activity bishops/ deacons were later co-opted. But the bishops/deacons here were not priests, and neither were the presbyters who are elsewhere mentioned in the saga of evolving Christian leadership. In fact, when institutionalizing of these leadership roles did occur and presbyters were allowed to preside at the Eucharist instead of bishops, which at first they were not allowed to do, they needed no 'ordination' in order to fill this new role. In the first three centuries or so the title 'priest' was seldom applied, and then only to the bishop and only allegorically. Thereafter, the process by which Christianity came to distinguish a hierarchical priesthood, wherein  the bishop/presbyter is different in *status* and not just different in the variety of roles played in the community of equals, makes a long and complex story. What matters is that it owes a great deal to the adoption of the different 'orders' of secular Roman society and nothing at all to institution by Jesus. The process by which members of this priestly caste then came to be considered possessors of special 'sacred power' is equally complex and even longer— Schillebeeckx argues that the concept of 'sacred power' belongs really to the second millennium of Christianity's history—and undoubtedly connected with the increasingly restricted attribution of the real presence of the body of Christ to the 'words of consecration'.

The implications of this revision of the Roman Catholic foundation myth are many and wide. The Last Supper was not an ordination ceremony for the first Christian priest-bishops. Even if the accounts of it near the close of each of the four gospels are in the main historical—and few scholars would now doubt that these accounts were heavily influenced by subsequent liturgical practice—and even if we could be sure that Mark's Twelve were present rather than John's uncounted 'disciples', there is still nothing to suggest that the symbolic role of the Twelve is not still the paramount one, so that the 'do this in remembrance' is addressed to the whole community of the new Israel. Nothing in the scene denotes the special conferring of sacred power or the creation of a clerical estate, and there is no sign of such in the early communities after the death of Jesus. The institution by Jesus of such a hierarchical and ministerial priesthood, in which the word priesthood connotes something different in essence from what it connotes when used allegorically of all the faithful, is wholly a creation of the foundation myth in the form which it later came to acquire.

Indeed it is not irrelevant to mention here that the view of the Last Supper as an ordination ceremony for the first Christian priest-bishops (and, of course, priest-pope) is closely bound to the view of the Last Supper as the occasion on which the Eucharist itself was instituted. But this view is itself highly suspect and without sufficient foundation in the New Testament. Furthermore, it is only by paying the closest attention to what the New Testament has to say about Jesus' table-fellowship during his public ministry that one can discover what is truly distinctive about this symbolic meal. Concentration on cultic priesthood and sacred power simply distracts from this.

What comes into focus here, as in the general scanning of Christian sources for the emerging shape of leadership, is the primacy of community, not in the cosy sense of the tea-party with which it is too often confused, but in the sense of the astonishing, indeed revolutionary, equality of all under the newly understood reign of God. The community was apostolic in its living, celebrating, and preaching the gospel, and its in-dwelling spirit provided it with those who would lead it in any form of activity in which it needed to engage. The growing need to institutionalize and centralize some of these forms of leadership could not deprive the community itself of its primary responsibilities and consequent rights. Hence, in the case of Eucharistic celebration, as in the case of 'apostolicity' of doctrine or general practice, if the community celebrates the Eucharist in the distinctive form which Jesus gave it, then its eucharistic presidents or ministers are 'valid'. No Eucharist is made 'valid' by a mythical sequence of laying on of hands going back unbroken to 'the Twelve'.

The preceding analysis must not be construed as an attack upon the eucharistic ministry of any church; quite the contrary. The lesson to be learned here is comparable to the lesson learned from looking at the emergent ecclesiastical institutions in general. The varied eucharistic ministries in the Christian churches that we know all have equal claim to validity, and none needs to be validated by officers of another church. If a community is eucharistic in the spirit of Jesus it can provide the presidency that it needs for its Eucharistic celebration. Nor is the preceding analysis an attack upon the Roman Catholic priesthood or upon the pertinent part of the Roman Catholic foundation myth and the truth which in the distinctive manner of myth this part seeks to claim. Of course Roman Catholics can continue to accept their present priesthood as presidency of their eucharistic celebrations, entrusted with the duty to see that the Eucharist is regularly and properly celebrated by its celebrant, the community. Meanwhile the powerful symbolism of the unbroken line of laid-on hands makes the claim that, in this church, the Lord's Supper is celebrated as the Lord celebrated it with his first disciples—just as the same symbolism claims in other parts of the foundation myth that his truth is still preached and his way still followed.

What Roman Catholics cannot do, even if they were soon to get the support of Eastern Orthodox and Anglicans for this, is to use their myth to deny the validity of other Christian forms of church government and church ministry and in this way to continue to hinder the modern ecumenical movement. For that is the point at which people really are tempted either to look to an invisible church for the true church of Christ or to think that the true church must be brought into being again through institutional initiatives, through alterations or realignments in ecclesiastical government. There is no invisible church, and it is a total travesty of that hierarchy of Christian truths to which Vatican II itself refers to have something as essential as Christain unity made to wait upon something as optional as forms of ecclesiastical government and related institutions of ministry. Yet Roman Catholics do in fact do just what I say they cannot do, in documents emanating from just those institutions I have been analysing!

## The modern ecumenical movement

Jesus' own prayer for unity (John 17: 20 ff.), the prayer most frequently recited by all who wish to express their own unconditional dedication to this worthy cause, is found at the opening of the Decree on Papal Primacy from the Fourth Session of Vatican I. This should raise no eyebrows, for the Final Report of the Anglican-Roman Catholic International Commission proposes an acceptable form of papal primacy for some future reunion of these churches; the present incumbent of the See of Rome has highest on his own version of the ecumenical agenda some mutual understanding with the Greeks; and, most important of all, to this day no official document of the Roman Catholic Church has ever given the impression that reunion can be achieved other than by the acceptance by other churches of some form of papal primacy and then, presumably, of the kind of hierarchical institutions of which papacy is surely the paradigm.

Nowhere is this last point clearer than in Vatican II's Decree on Ecumenism. It is of some incidental interest to note that the then Pope, Paul VI, intervened personally several times in the final drafting of that decree; on every occasion his intervention hardened the Roman position, and on every occasion his authority was allowed to prevail. But the document itself is crystal clear, and some brief quotation is sufficient to put its position in view. The result of belated Roman Catholic ecumenical action 'will be that, little by little, as the obstacles to perfect ecclesiastical communion are overcome, all Christians will be gathered, in a common celebration of the Eucharist, into that unity of the one and only church which Christ bestowed on his church from the beginning. This unity, we believe, dwells in the Catholic church as something she can never lose' (par. 4). And lest anyone should be in any doubt about the precise identity of this one and only church which possesses this unity, the previous paragraph had explained that 'our separated brethren, whether considered as individuals or as communities and churches, are not blessed with that unity which Christ wished to bestow'. Rather, the paragraph continues, 'it was to the apostolic college alone, of which Peter is the head, that we believe our Lord entrusted all the blessings of the New Covenant, in order to establish on earth the one Body of Christ into which all those should be fully incorporated who already belong in any way to God's People'.

The most well-meaning of ecumenists do their cause no good by seeking to blur the harsh outline of this position. Some quote the sentence from Vatican II's Constitution 'On The Church' which says that the unique church of Christ 'subsists' in the Catholic Church, and in premature and slightly pathetic triumph they add: you see, it does not say that the one church of Christ *is* the Roman Catholic Church! They thereby ignore the power of the word 'subsists' in the scholastic jargon of Roman Catholic officialdom, but more seriously they ignore what must be plain to all who read the sentence in its context, namely, that this verb is chosen in this context to allow for the admission that elements of sanctification and truth do exist in other Christian churches, while insisting that these very elements 'possess an inner dynamism towards Catholic unity' (par. 8). That is to say, their inner force is to bring people back to Rome. More pathetic still are efforts to avoid the clear import of Roman Catholic doctrine by drawing attention to Roman Catholic statements about the pilgrim nature of Christian community life, to the fact that other Christian bodies are, after all, called churches or at least ecclesial communions, and so on. All this merely fudges the fact that Rome does not envisage reunion, and in particular it does not envisage eucharistic communion, until the institutional issue has been resolved in terms which it will find acceptable: in terms, that still seems to mean, of its own foundation myth.

'The more we meet as brothers and sisters in the love of Christ, the less we are able to tolerate not being able to share together in the great mystery of the Eucharist.' These words were spoken by Pope John Paul II to his Secretariat for Promoting Christian Unity on 18 November 1978. Why, with the very few exceptions which Roman Catholic rules make for what is quaintly called intercommunion, does he still think we must all tolerate this pain? Well, despite the fact that Roman Catholics pray in the Prayer after Communion for the 11th Sunday in Ordinary Time: 'Lord, may this Eucharist accomplish in your church the unity and peace which it signifies'—or, perhaps I should say, because the Roman authorities take it that the unity Christ promised is already present in the Roman Catholic Church and simply needs the return of the others to perfect it—the principle is laid down that Eucharist is the expression of unity achieved rather than a means towards unity desired. It follows from this that where unity is insufficient, intercommunion may not be allowed.

A brief scan of the Roman Catholic *Ecumenical Directory*[3] would reveal that there are two main kinds of unity in which defects may occur: church unity, which seems to mean unity at the institutional ministerial level, and unity in faith, in what different Christian groups believe, specifically but by no means exclusively about the Eucharist. In the matter of institutional church unity and validity of ordained ministry, spokesmen for the Orthodox churches seem to echo the Roman Catholic position, so it is no surprise to learn that intercommunion is most freely allowed between these two; Anglicans seem to be more divided, and Rome has not of course rescinded its declaration that Anglican orders are 'absolutely null and utterly void'. The ministers of many of the other churches of the Reformation invite to the Lord's table any who love or seek to follow the Lord, though many in these churches would not dream of taking part in the 'blasphemy' of the Roman Mass.

## Unity in faith

In the matter of unity in faith, those interested in discovering deficiencies may find their task a good deal more difficult. It we leave out of account official positions taken on the matter of institution and ministry, what is surely most remarkable about the contemporary scene is the extraordinary growth of theological consensus, and theology in every church represents its developing understanding of the faith. From today's theology tomorrow's preaching, indeed tomorrow's official teaching, will come; that is sure, even if some days are longer than others and some tomorrows take longer to come, and even though the vast bulk of any day's theology does not survive the night. The consensus achieved in modern theology is best found if one looks in the least obvious places: not in deliberately designed ecumenical institutes but in the everyday work of theological faculties which are the better for preserving a traditional church allegiance while they quietly pursue their critical studies and in doing so assimilate all worthwhile contributions without noticing *their* particular ecclesiastical provenance.

The consensus which is most immediately relevant in this particular context is that achieved between representatives of all the main Christian churches on the theology of Eucharist. In general and fundamental areas of belief in God and in Jesus our common faith is often pointed out with pride, but even in the particular area of the theology of the Eucharist, it would be very difficult indeed to argue successfully that there is still such deficient agreement in faith as to justify postponing broad intercommunion on these grounds. In 1977, five years after the Anglican-Roman Catholic International Commission had produced an agreed document on the Eucharist, the then Archbishop of Canterbury and the then Pope jointly declared that 'the moment will shortly come when the respective authorities must evaluate the conclusions'.[4] Eight years later that moment shows no signs of coming. That is but one example of unexplained procrastination following upon remarkable theological agreement. One cannot but conclude that of the three elements which make up a religion, its doctrine (creed and code), its ritual and its institutions, it is the tragic insistence on placing the last before the other two, and particularly before the rich and powerful sacramental celebration, that threatens to keep Christianity today on its divisive and self-destructive path. The last service which modern theology can render to the institutional leaders of the various churches is to point out to them the limited though real value of their foundation myths and the great damage that is caused when the limited truth of these myths is exceeded and abused. Once that is done any further hindrance placed by institutional leaders on the cause of Christian union will be entirely their own responsibility.

## A plan for Christian union

Theology itself, however, does not as yet appear to be willing to draw out the fullest implications of its own growing consensus both on the origins of office and ministry in the church and on the nature and importance of the Eucharist. If I take here the example of a recent book by the Roman Catholic theologians Heinrich Fries and Karl Rahner, it is only because my remarks, for reasons already given, have so far centred on the Roman Catholic foundation myth. The book by Fries and Rahner is entitled *Union of the Churches: A Real Possibility*. Convinced that the urgency of union has increased dramatically in the contemporary world, and that it is now a real possibility, the authors present a plan for its accomplishment. They feel that there is sufficient doctrinal basis for union in the foundational truths of Christianity as these are expressed in Scripture, the Apostles' Creed and the Nicene (Constantinopolitan) Creed, and that beyond these foundational truths no member of the united churches should deliberately denounce a mandatory doctrine of another church or require another church's confession of one of its dogmas. Furthermore, in the aftermath of union the churches could be expected to seek and find more doctrinal agreement within their traditional formulae—for such has been the bulk of theological experience in the recent ecumenical climate. They feel that there is no great problem about the united churches each keeping its own institutional structure, albeit often sharing the same territory.

The authors do, however, believe that all uniting churches must recognize the 'Petrine ministry' of the Bishop of Rome, though they envisage that the exercise of this primacy would need to be more collegial and to devolve more responsibility than ever before, and that it should in fact bind itself solemnly to recognize the traditional structures of the uniting churches. They do nevertheless require the uniting churches to have bishops at the head of their larger subdivisions, if they do not already have them, though they allow that the choice of these bishops need not be quite so much under Roman thumbs as is presently the case in the Roman Catholic Church. (Papal confirmation of the results of local elections might suffice?) In addition, all uniting churches would be required to bind themselves to ordination of ministers by prayer and the laying on of hands so as to make recognition of such ordination possible to the Roman Catholic Church. It is not altogether clear to this reader of the Fries-Rahner plan what exactly happens next. It seems as if existing ministers whose ordination is presently invalid in Roman Catholic eyes could have their ministry 'validated' by some global Catholic recognition during the act of union. The result envisaged clearly is this: that since there is at this stage sufficient community in both faith and institutions, intercommunion could at last be possible.

Now it is not right to dismiss out of hand any plan for reunion, or any of the many reports of joint commissions which have tried in their various ways to bring that reunion nearer. Nor could it be right to deny that reunion round the Table of the Lord is the consummate instance of that reunion, for nothing gives the lie to the Christian message in this world so much as the refusal to break bread. But it is surely right to cast a quizzical look at the place in the order of ideal events which even this bold plan allots to intercommunion. Once again it is last, after all the political negotiations about institutions and ministries, appointments and recognitions—as if these were the source of Christ's power in the world, as if Christ's real and healing presence in this world had to wait upon their concordats. One only has to state it to see how ludicrous it is!

## Eucharist as the key to achieving unity

The prominence of the ecumenical theme in this chapter might lead one to believe that the main point was prudential: Christians are now a minority in a post-Christian world and Christianity will succumb to the combined hostile forces of communism and secularism, and to the attraction of other religions, unless Christians can somehow manage to present a united front. But that is not the point—if only because Christians need a far more positive appreciation of humanism and of other religions than such a point could imply. The point of this chapter is the search for what the followers of Jesus have from earliest times called the body of Christ, and hence for the ways in which the spirit of Jesus is still embodied in the world, if it *is* still embodied in the world, and for some sense of priorities amongst these if, as is likely, they are many. The argument in this as in earlier chapters is that the spirit of Jesus is primarily embodied in this world in the Eucharist, where the story of God's mighty deeds culminating in his action in Jesus is told and where people break for each other the bread of life. This ritual is *the* proclamation, as Paul called it. In it people can be exposed to the spirit of Jesus and so experience his real presence, for the Lord, as Paul again put it, is life-giving spirit. A community, large or small, is a true Christian community if it properly celebrates this ritual; in ecclesiastical jargon, it is then apostolic. Then, too, its formal institutions and ministries are apostolic.

The same could be said about the formal teaching in which all Christian communities engage: if it does in fact propose the truth about Jesus, then the communities concerned and their official teachers are to that extent also apostolic. But the Eucharistic criterion has priority because formal teaching is subservient to the drama in which divinity is encountered and to the story told in the drama, both of which formal teaching must simply seek to explain. Historical hypothesis and evidence, logical analysis and argument, take place within the imaginative vision and its dramatic representation, and can never become a substitute for them.

Hence it is not the forms of institutions—the ecclesiastical structures as they are called, the various constitutional shapes of ministry—that determine the truth, the apostolicity, of a community. Nor is it, in the first instance, the formal teaching: it is necessary to state this explicitly, for episcopal hierarchies in particular have a habit of using the need for orthodox doctrine as a means of arguing that Jesus must have directly instituted *their* magisterium, when in actual fact he did not. It is the eucharistic experience, in the broadest understanding of that phrase, that can keep the teaching orthodox, and the community is celebrant of the Eucharist. The community evolved its varied offices or institutionalized ministries to oversee this process on its behalf and to take responsibility in its name for its faithful continuance; and the spirit of Jesus which breathes in the eucharistic community supplies it still with the less institutionalized charismatics —the apostles and prophets, the teachers and healers, the visionaries and martyrs, who are equally necessary for its fidelity to the founder.

The primary point of the argument, then, is this: since the Eucharist is the primordial embodiment of the spirit of Jesus in the world it is to the Eucharist that Christians, all Christians, must first go in order to have that spirit in them which is also in Christ Jesus. Any 'officer' who prevents Christians from participating in a Eucharist celebrated by another Christian church, especially when the best theological endeavours have shown the same faith in Christ's real presence in both churches, is not only acting *ultra vires*, he is actively propounding a false view of Christianity. The damage done within Christianity is then a far more serious matter than the damage done by the divided image it presents to the world at large. It is more serious even than the appallingly inhuman damage that is done to Christian couples who, as the crass phrase has it, enter a mixed marriage, and to their children. That the Christian faith, and in particular the Christian Eucharist, should be used to drive a wedge into the very symbol of Christ's union with the church, represents of course an inexcusable assault upon the family, but that is because it represents an even more serious misunderstanding of the nature of Christianity itself. As a result we have a new generation of children lost to Christianity because they see through the posturing of all the institutional churches, and the unwillingness of so many of their most vociferous adherents to engage together in the most elementary Christian action of the breaking of bread. But we also have an increasing number of young people who continue to call themselves Christian, refuse to declare their allegiance to any of the separated churches, and partake of the Eucharist wherever they wish. These obviously hold out more hope, and although their solution is far from the ideal as yet, they serve to remind us of one final feature of the kind of argument in which we are here engaged.

It is all too easy in these closing stages of the argument to be led into the old temptation of laying the blame on church leaders. And this, of course, would be just another way of propagating that false view of the Christian community which the body of the argument was anxious to correct. But if the Eucharist is the primary embodiment of the power and presence of Jesus in the world, and if the Christian community is celebrant of the Eucharist, then it is primarily the responsibility of the Christian community-at-large to break bread together in any and every local church which the community can recognize to be celebrating a true sacrament of unity in the spirit of Jesus. Community officers, as the common name 'ministers' suggests, are there to serve the communities in this their essential activity.

The key to the immediate progress of ecumenism, which is widely thought to have entered the doldrums, is contained in the Eucharist, because in the Eucharist is the principal source of the power to heal the broken and to reconcile the estranged. I could no longer think of bringing up my children in the belief that only Roman Catholics and Eastern Orthodox celebrated 'valid' Eucharist; and the suggestion that other churches in celebrating the Eucharist have not, in words inserted by Paul VI in the Decree on Ecumenism, preserved the genuine reality of the Eucharistic mystery, but do nevertheless enjoy 'spiritual' communion with the body of Jesus, I consider to be a pusillanimous piece of theological evasion from people who still lack the consistency or the courage to draw attention to the fullest implications of the main movements in modern theology, and to question the unjustified primacy of ecclesiastical office.

Does all this mean ecclesiastical anarchy? It does not. The Roman Catholic Church, in my case, is my spiritual home. It is in constant need of reformation, as is every other church. But I would not leave it or be put out of it, and I would naturally hope that my children would continue to feel a similar *pietas* towards it. The new worldwide community of Christians, who show by their immediate willingness to break bread with each other the true healing and reconciling power of the Eucharist on this tragic earth, will preserve the rich plurality of forms of Christian life by carrying forward each its own precious heritage of practice, language, and structure. The new openness of all their tables will enable their mutual appreciation and their mutual enrichment. There is no real fear of a standardized and deadening uniformity coming about in this way; the religious imagination is far too vital a faculty. Some people will continue to change churches, of course, but this they have always done. The only *caveat* will be the one which has always existed, that such changes be contemplated only in deepest conscience and after the most careful and lengthy consideration, for powerful spiritual heritages cannot be exchanged lightly without the greatest of spiritual loss. But all the

odium hitherto attached to suspicions of proselytizing and deriv-
ing from rival claims to be the one true church of Christ will be at
an end; for the visible church, the body of Christ in the world,
will consist of all the Christians in the world, all in Eucharistic
communion, and its physical skeleton will be the openness of all
tables to all.

It is true that Christianity is more than Eucharist, though
Eucharist is its most essential expression, and so further forms of
this new union will also be found. Some are already well under
way in the area of faith. Theological consensus is well advanced,
and dialogue continues; the sharing of pulpits, by which Christians of different churches proclaim the good news to each other,
is widely and frequently accepted. At the institutional level also
the new union will find increasingly more adequate modes of
expression. It is possible that a Petrine function, based upon the
See of Rome, might some day be able to act as the centre of
Christian unity in the world, but that would need such a radical
change in the present theory and practice of papacy that there is
no prospect of it happening in the foreseeable future.

Nor is it necessary. Neither Scripture nor the earliest apostolic
traditions required it; and the world has long outgrown the
emperor ideal, where one man embodied as a kind of corporate
person the whole people. The papacy might possibly remain a
feature of the institution of Western Catholicism. An institution
such as the World Council of Churches is quite adequate to the
task of providing the forum within which churches large and
local scattered round the world can show their care for each
other, and it can then function as a focus of charity. Institutional
matters are always secondary to and more optional than matters
of practice and matters of faith, and they are not themselves
matters of faith.

This chapter should not end without one final critical comment
upon that theology of Eucharist which sees Eucharist as the
expression of unity achieved rather than the powerful sacrament
which can bring unity to estranged people through its reconciling
symbols. Whatever differences there may still be between the
major Christian churches in their theological accounts of the real
presence of Jesus in the Eucharist, that very phrase which they

# 6

# The Ways of the World

There may have been a time, and that not so long ago, when Christians could have rested satisfied, for a while at least, with an acceptable vision of a united Christianity. But that time is already past. Today any image of united Christianity simply sets in greater relief the counter-image of divided humanity, divided as much as anything else by religious affiliations or by ideologies which seem to have all the force of the religions they successfully sought to replace. It can be no accident that so many of the warring parties in the world today are identified by their religious allegiances: Catholics and Protestants in Northern Ireland might cease to fight if Christian unity became real, but what of Christians, Jews, and Muslims in Lebanon, Hindus and Sikhs in India . . .

Nowadays one cannot pause even for a moment before the vision of a united Christianity; the world we know demands immediate attention to the problem of the unity of humankind across all religions and ideologies. Yet this demand in turn sets the question about the essence of Christianity back into focus once again. Just how open can its eucharistic table be? Just how far can its recently advertised challenge to the distinction between secular and sacred be allowed to go? And will such openness and such challenge to divisive distinctions, whatever their extent, help or hinder *rapprochement* with rival religions and rival ideologies?

## Religious faith and the religions

Other religions and ideologies of course have their own formulae for relating to their rivals, or for avoiding or dissolving any such relationships, and the first thing to strike the enthusiastic enquirer after some possible unity for the human race is the depressing fact that these formulae are themselves very different, both within and between religions.

A Marxist ideology—for Marx's work did in the hands of his followers become an ideology—would dispel the divisions caused by different religions by ushering in the end of all religion, and any other divisions would be overcome by the conversion of the whole human race to the one ideology. Such is the doctrinaire solution implicitly espoused by all those forms of reductionism with which the end of the last century and the beginning of this one were replete. And since this kind of solution is nothing more nor less than ideological imperialism in thin disguise, it can scarcely avoid the obvious hazards for humankind of all forms of imperialism: the intolerance, the coercion, the persecution, all flowering from sheer lack of respect for the most deeply held convictions of other human beings.

The odd thing about the modern reductionists, the Marxists, the Freudians, the Durkheimians, and all those more generally in awe before the face of modern science, is that they repeated so woodenly the mistake so often made by so many religious people: they took the doctrine, the theory, to be the reality with which they were primarily concerned, and they allowed the theory to control their experience of the reality, thus preferring conceptual control to practical imagination. In this way they too often shackled the liberating force of their own original revelations, and became so like the doctrinaire religions they sought to depose that the human race was left with some very bleak options indeed. To take some examples from psychology: B. F. Skinner's *Beyond Freedom and Dignity* is already quite passé, but is Philip Rieff's formula for 'sweetening the time' in *The Triumph of the Therapeutic* any more reassuring? Surely not.

At least Ernest Becker's *The Denial of Death* attempted to make allowance for the human being's apparently ineradicable passion for infinity. Becker's God, the supreme transference object of puny people ridden by annihilation anxiety, may be remote and seemingly indifferent. Indeed the issue of the very existence of Becker's God may share in the pervasive sense of ambiguity so often spread these days by poets like Wallace Stevens, who want to be counted atheists in the jargon of the philosophy of religion and yet wish to be left open to something wondrous in the world, some 'source', something worthy of belief, without which their poetic imaginations would seize up on a dry diet of empirical fact. But in spite of all that is off-putting or ambiguous here, at least a depth of the human spirit is being addressed, a depth which all the best-advertised reductionist philosophies have simply failed to reach, a depth which so much that passes for religion may also have failed to satisfy, but at least did *not* fail to reach.

There is something that borders upon intellectual dishonesty in people whose powerful imaginations bring them to the depths of ordinary experience in the world at which the less dogmatic religious people recognize the beginnings of the religious quest, while they evade the metaphysical questions there entailed or, more superficially still, want to play with traditional religious imagery while dressing up ostentatiously in the plain white uniform of the modern atheist. There is something that borders upon the morally irresponsible about people who seek either to ignore or to enlist on the side of their reductionist systems the deep passion for absolutes which has always driven this very driven race, and which religions have tried to channel into a quest for some still distant goodness, truth, and beauty.

Of course, the concept of a religion is itself a problematic one. Some of what are now considered distinct religions were once comprehensive ways of life, encompassing all the levels at which life is lived, from the most superficial to the deepest. They had no particular name and hence carried no suggestion that they might represent only a part of life, however honoured a part that might be. This was true of Hinduism, for example. In some other cases, men now regarded as founders of distinct religions had themselves no intention of founding a 'new' religion. This was almost certainly true of Jesus; and the Buddha, Gautama Siddartha, according to the introductory lectures of Irmgard Schloegl, insisted that he had done no more than rediscover an ancient way to an ancient city. Yet other religions seem to have been designed for the specific purpose of overcoming divisions which had developed, with the usual tragic consequences, between established religions. This was true of Guru Nanak and the Sikh religion.

But, in spite of all such factors, a combination of cultural differentiation in the course of history with natural human chauvinism brought about in time the mutual ignorance, the suspicion, and incipient fear which ignorance breeds, and the incubating hostility which so frequently characterizes religious divisions in the world today. And it is to this sorry scene that religions add different and irreconcilable formulae for regulating their own relationships.

## The problem of exclusivism

Within many religions the harsh exclusivist call is sounded by one or more parties. Usually it sounds as harshly at the approach of other parties in the same religion as it does for outsiders. Many a Protestant Christian proves more intolerant of a Roman Catholic than of a Hindu or a Muslim. The pathetic little fortress mentality feeds as much upon fears of the spirit as upon fears of the body; the same groundless dread builds similar fortress-prisons for both, and the same persistent calls for loyalty keep the walls erect against a wider freedom and a larger truth. Between Christianity and other religions the exclusivist note was sounded early on by the truculent Tertullian—what has Athens to do with Jerusalem?—and much more recently by the fastidious Barth. 'We Christians,' Barth declared in his *Dogmatics in Outline*, 'speak of Him who completely takes the place of everything that elsewhere is usually called "God", and therefore suppresses and excludes it all, and claims to be alone the truth.' 'God in the sense of the Christian confession,' he adds, 'is and exists in a completely different way from that which is elsewhere called divine.'[1]

There are logical and linguistic problems here. Difference is only perceptible where there is some similarity: 'complete difference' is therefore inconceivable; and God is a noun rather than a proper name. The context of these quotes is one in which Barth's phobia before natural theology is particularly prominent. (One is reminded of Marx's shrewd observation: 'theologians establish two kinds of religion. Every religion which is not their own is an invention of man, and hence artificial, while their own comes from God.'[2]) Barth certainly wrote better pages. That being said, all we need from him here is an expression of Christian exclusivism, and that he certainly offers us. Similarly exclusivist claims are made by parties within both Judaism and Islam. Indeed it would be interesting to know if such claims were more characteristic of monotheistic religions than they are of other world religions—although, of course, one must remember however, that there are always those in all religious parties who resist the exclusivist claims.

However—and this must be said at the very outset—it is difficult to assess the real import of the more open-minded statements made by religious people about other religions; indeed it is sometimes difficult to avoid the impression that they represent a form of imperial intent which is all the more insidious because it is so well disguised from speaker and listener alike. In similar manner the leading powers in the self-styled 'free world' complain of communist tactics of using their armed forces to enforce loyalty in satellite countries, while they themselves keep the world 'free' for a kind of 'free' capitalist enterprise which economically enslaves millions in the poorer countries—and poverty, as Gandhi said, is the worst form of violence. If a Christian extends to all peoples everywhere the latitude shown by the author of Hebrews to his own forebears; if he allows that God's revelation is present in all other religions, but regards all this as the *preparatio evangelica*, the divine preparation for the (Christian) gospel, he is surely interpreting the immutable divine intent as the eventual shepherding of all people into the Christian fold. And if a Jew, in one of his more universalist moods, insists that God's revelation to his people was not for that people's exclusive use and benefit but was, on the contrary, given as a light to all the Gentiles, does he not mean that all people should eventually become Jews or Jewish 'God-fearers', at least to the extent of accepting the Jewish version of God's nature and providence? Islam maintains an openness to all 'people of the Book', which means that those who truly follow previous prophets, Abraham or Jesus, are regarded as true Muslims, truly obedient to the one God's eternal will which found definitive historical expression in the Holy Qur'an; furthermore the revelation in the Qur'an was given, not for any restricted ethnic group, but for all people everywhere. Does this mean that we should all of us eventually obey all the prescriptions of the Qur'an and, if not all, then which ones?

A Hindu spokesman once told me that if I followed the *Samanya Dharma*, the generally applicable values of *ahimsa*—truthfulness, non-coveting, purity, and control of the sense appetites—I would be to him a Hindu, no matter what the forms in which I worshipped the one formless, eternal spirit from whom the whole universe came. I must return to *ahimsa* later, and I realize that truthfulness can involve the revelation of metaphysical depths rather than simply the avoidance of telling lies. But the only point I need to make here is that my interlocutor was following the conviction of his faith that Hinduism is not a particular religion, it is a spiritual discipline or way. He would have accepted a traditional Hindu metaphor which decribes the different religions of the world as differently shaped vessels in which different peoples carried from the one sacred river the same water of life. But I still wonder if this most open of religious views of other religions does not in itself convey a very particular idea of the nature of religion which other religions might with some justification regard as an imposition rather than in any acceptable sense a formula for unity in plurality.

The view of a Buddhist spokesman, Roshi Daishin, might well be found more acceptable. He said that, although each person should try to find the way that rang true for him or her, and none who finally engaged with a Zazen master like himself might express anything but reverence and gratitude for any former religious allegiance, the Zazen way would lead to enlightenment and consummate joy only those who, once embarked upon it, followed it to the end with implicit trust, never deviating to any other way. For there is something Platonic, in one popular sense of the word, about a view of religion which can distil its essence as easily as the Hindu metaphor does from all its historical manifestations, as easily as the differing shapes of the vessels can be distinguished from the common water they contain; as if religion, like water, could be poured from one historical container to another without the slightest alteration to its substance.

The case is no different when we use terminology after the manner of Cantwell-Smith and call the religions the vessels and faith the water; or when we speculate with the imprisoned Bonhoeffer that Christianity might not be a religion in that sense of the word at all. For faith is never a disembodied spirit, a pure Platonic form. It is always incarnate in the words and actions of people of particular times and places. It seems, then, that other religions, and the relatively new discipline of comparative religion/religious studies, will have to wrestle with the problems of faith and history, as Christianity has begun to wrestle with them over the course of the last two centuries. For history, the discipline, focuses upon the particularities of embodiment at different times and places. In addition if brings into permanent view history, the reality, the progress (or regress) of praxis, within which religions, through their actual representatives, actually relate to each other in ways which often ignore and sometimes contradict the formal proposals for those relationships outlined above.

This does not mean that we should put aside any of the formal proposals about relationships between religions outlined above, or any others not included in that short list. For these do represent accounts of the ways in which people believe they should relate to followers of other faiths. It is simply necessary to note that they all of them betray, in their different ways, the proponent's belief in the truth of the religion to which he or she belongs.

Indeed we should expect no less, for it would be odd indeed if someone were to profess allegiance to a faith while having reservations about the prospects it held for reaching the truth, however obvious might be the failures in that truth of any of its devotees past or present. The best that we can hope for at the level of formal declaration, then, is that these varied ways of asserting the truth of each one's religious position will always be accompanied by the unwavering conviction that one's version of the truth should be offered to others freely but that these others should never be in any way coerced to consider it, much less to accept it; and, in the case of the more open-minded statements, that the one who offers his or her version of the truth to others should also be open to improvement from the revelations of other religions.

## The role of praxis

But all this still remains at the formal level of conceptualized beliefs about relationships between conceptualized faiths. The point of bringing concrete history and praxis back into consideration was not simply to sustain to the end a central theme of this book, but to suggest that the modern forum in which the relationships between religions and alternative ideologies are being decided is once more the forum which is signposted by the practicalist thesis. It is indeed surprising to note the number of religions which describe themselves as 'ways'—and if Marx is to be taken at his word in his powerful proposal of the practicalist thesis, then Marxism also is a 'way' rather than an ideology. All this surely suggests that, just as the truth of any particular way lies not in its conceptual claims and their argued supports, but in its proven ability to lead humanity to a better condition, so the issue of the relationships between religions and between religions and comparable ideologies cannot be decided by conceptual claim and counter-claim. Instead it must face the acid test of practical amelioration or deterioration of the human condition—a test which in this case is most quickly and surely applied by simply observing how followers of one religion or ideology actually treat the followers of another.

If one were now to take this line of reasoning a step further and say that to compare ways is to compare moralities, protests would undoubtedly converge upon one's innocent head from different directions. Humanists, whether they be Marxist humanists or not, would no doubt protest that true morality must be kept immune from the corrupting effects of religion. And they might find some partial allies amongst some religious writers. In the course of the much-debated question: is there a Christian morality, some Christian writers argue that there certainly is, if only because it would otherwise be difficult to see how Christianity could make a distinctive contribution to the affairs of everyday living. Other Christian writers, however, more sensitive perhaps to the real problems of everyday life in an increasingly pluralist, polarized, yet shrinking world, would prefer to say that morality is generally accessible to believers and non-believers alike; that religious faith may supply a high inspiration to be moral but does not define the content of moral duty. Otherwise, they ask, how could the kind of universal moral co-operation ever be possible, upon which the fate of humanity increasingly depends?

It is the latter kind of Christian writer who is most likely to be embarrassed by those relics of religious establishment in which officers of a faith still attempt to impose their moral precepts upon increasingly secularized societies. The precise political means by which this is attempted are not in themselves of prime significance. Sometimes the institutions of government may be used, especially where, as in the case of the Church of England, a church is still formally an established church. At other times *episcopoi*, overseers, may abjure all intention of seeking to suborn the offices of State but, as happens in the Republic of Ireland, they will not hesitate to apply the three-line whip to every pulpit in the land which falls under their control when a moral issue which interests them comes to the vote. In this more indirect but no less effective manner they can have their politically neutral cake and eat it. Shades of Constantinian Christianity, ghost of Christendom, lengthening shadow of the post-Reformation Treaty of Westphalia and its *cuius regio eius et religio*: a person's religious affiliation coincides in more than one way with the political region in which he or she resides.

Once again, whatever the formal theories about the relationship between religion and morality, in practice religious communities do constantly attempt to shape ethical attitudes, and indeed the whole of moral life, in the territories in which they have achieved some dominance, and this includes political actions and attitudes. One thinks of the Moral Majority and its more recent successor in the United States of America, and of Christian Liberation movements in Latin America, but one is not of course confined to Christian examples. Muslim *Shariah* is designed for whole political communities, as the recent Islamic revival in some Middle Eastern countries has made abundantly clear; and an orthodox Jewish rabbi in the Israeli Knesset would acknowledge no separation of Church and State. It is therefore impossible in practice to avoid taking a position on the relationship between religion and morality, however attractive in theory the closing of their frontiers might be.

As soon as one looks to praxis, then, instead of continuing these more rarified arguments, one can scarcely avoid being struck by the fact that in this belligerent world there would appear to be quite a number of causes of a quite disparate nature for which people are prepared to die, or to kill, or at the very least to risk their own lives while threatening the lives of others. This apparently permanent and most sinister feature of life upon this planet offers, I believe, a most dependable short-cut to an answer to an otherwise quite complex question—the question, that is, about the moral values by which particular peoples live. Indeed it might well lead us also to an answer to the question as to whether or not human morality can stop short of religious commitment.

## Can one have morality without religion?

In a book entitled simply *Religion*, the Polish philosopher Leszek Kolakowski, now a fellow of All Souls, Oxford, argues that rationalism, the bequest of the Enlightenment to late Western civilization, cannot support any moral value whatever (and Kolakowski is at the very least an agnostic). Nietzsche he takes as a source of one of the two forms of atheistic humanism which have recently emerged in the West (the other is Marxism), and as an example of one who was convinced that science had robbed the world and human history of sense. For, as Kolakowski himself insists, the discovery of the facts of the case, however much probability it can boast, can never provide the slightest infusion of human meaning, purpose, goal, or value. Those who would live by science and logic alone must therefore face an utterly indifferent universe, as a few consistent atheists of recent times have in fact managed to do. Kolakowski finds Nietzsche himself inconsistent. For Nietzsche urges us to oppose our human dignity by sheer act of will to 'the impersonal game of atoms', to the deaf and indifferent universe in which we shall disappear without trace. But, writes Kolakowski, 'he failed to explain where the value of dignity came from, why it should not be another self-deception or why we may rely upon it rather than commit suicide or go mad, as he himself would subsequently do'.[3] As far as

Kolakowski is concerned, then, moral values belong with religious commitment, and atheistic humanists, who can of course behave as morally as anyone else, are living off their inheritance from what is to them a recently deceased religion. Religious faith, he says, cannot prove itself by dint of reasoning any more than its inherent moral values can be proved, despite those religious spokespersons who attempt to ape the rationalists in their use of evidence and logic. But it still remains true that morality belongs with religious faith, and cannot grow on any other kind of soil.

I believe that Kolakowski is right, or almost right, about all of this, but I should prefer to argue the case from below rather than from the lofty height from which *Religion* surveys all recent (and not so recent) religions, rationalisms, and moralities. To pursue some purpose, to have some goal, to commit some fraction of life however small to its achievement, and thus to create value—for only then is value created—is to be carried beyond all actual and possible knowledge of the way things are. Moral value is the challenging chasm between what is and what forever ought to be . . .

But perhaps the word 'forever' has crept too soon into the argument, and we should walk where Kolakowski wants to run. It is probable that purposes and goals, and therefore values, do exist, the claims of which upon reality could be calculated even on the kind of corrigible knowledge we now possess. For though there is a chasm between what is and what ought to be, the ought makes a claim upon reality, upon a present and future world, a claim that what one ought to do may be possible. Indeed an ought cannot be sustained without the belief and the hope that a world can be as that which I feel I ought to achieve, as my value, imagines it. In such obvious ways is morality bound up with faith and hope. And yet there is a case for saying that not all faith and hope is religious; not all human faith and hope reach for forever-lands, eternities, absolute and infinite realities such as religions envisage. When Camus had dismissed God because of the obvious injustice of the universal death sentence which God had imposed, he soon realized the folly of shaking his fists at an empty heaven and entitled the main ethical section of *The Rebel*, significantly, 'Moderation and Excess'. Our goals must be moderate, he maintained. We must wager only for some truth against the universal falsehood. Otherwise we shall be torn apart in the conflict of absolutes, our deadly inheritance from dead religions.

Bertrand Russell took what he believed to be the modern scientist's view of reality: indifferent matter rolling on its relentless way, assuring one and all of extinction in a limited time-span. Yet he was convinced that human beings could defiantly introduce some worthwhile values, could entertain a sense of obligation to these, could support an ought in spite of the indifference of what is, and in face of imminent extintion. And in his more poetic moments he spoke of how these carefully calculated values, calculated on a limited life-span and innocent of any hankering after eternity or absolutes, could serve 'to enlighten our little day'.

I must confess to a strong residual feeling that such moderate agnostic or atheistic humanism is a possibility—indeed I suspect that very many people, and amongst them many nominal Christians, actually live by it. I do see that it could entail Rieff's suggestion, in *Triumph of the Therapeutic*, of the use of the methods of modern psychology to try to rid the human spirit of its need for absolutes, and to increase the modern means of 'sweetening the time'.

I know that such moderate humanism cannot really deal with death—'nothing more terrible, nothing more true', in Philip Larkin's words, as he dismissed the

> specious stuff that says *No rational being*
> *Can fear a thing it will not feel*, not seeing
> That this is what we fear—no sight, no sound,
> No touch or taste or smell, nothing to think with,
> Nothing to love or link with.
>
> ('Aubade')

And there is great danger in any system that deals with human beings but cannot really deal with death. I know too that Kolakowski would dismiss, and not without a modicum of erudite contempt, such careful calculation of restricted human goals upon the probabilities of empirical knowledge, arguing no doubt that such measured expense of life upon such calculable results is no more than a poor utilitarian substitute for true morality. But it is simply too familiar a feature of life as it is lived to dimiss it entirely, and the argument does remain that, poor and comparatively contemptible as it is, it may well be preferable to those terrible, insatiable absolutes which have so often been foisted upon us both by religions and by so many of their secular substitutes, by Christians, Muslims, Jews, communists and fascists, and by those much more effective, if anonymous, people whose absolute value is profit.

It is fair to observe, however, that the project of calculating such modest values as might make life worthwhile, though they decline the challenge of meeting the threat of death, faces a double hazard. The first hazard is the simpler: it is the hazard of depending upon a certain length of time in order to achieve even a modest aim in life, a worthwhile and fulfilling career in the civil service, say, or the even simpler joys of having one's own family. This hazard arises because death is looked on as an event in the future, an end-point of life, problematic only because its date is normally unknown, or at least uncertain. But death, one must repeat, is much more than that. It is the enemy within. It lurks in the darkness of the human consciousness like one of those mythic monsters of the deep, and it breeds a fear which is like no other fear. As the existentialists pointed out, ordinary fears, however great, always relate to specific objects, but there is a kind called dread or anguish which has no describable object. When philosophers talk loftily about being and nothingness and the veil of nothingness through which we come upon such comprehensive concepts as 'being' or 'world', they are really talking about the homely awareness of death which colours all human experience —death being the peculiarly human form of the presence of nothingness; they are referring to the fact that all human awareness of everything is somewhere at its depth an awareness of incessant annihilation working patiently just beneath the fragile surfaces of things.

Gerard Manley Hopkins begins his poem 'Spring and Fall' 'to a young child' who is grieving over dying autumn leaves,

> Margaret, are you grieving
> Over Goldengrove unleaving?

and he ends with the lines,

> Now no matter, child, the name:
> Sorrow's springs are the same.
> Nor mouth had, no nor mind, expressed
> What heart heard of, ghost guessed:
> It is the blight man was born for,
> It is Margaret you mourn for.[4]

One line in the poem is remarkably reminiscent of Paul's 'eye hath not seen nor ear heard', and the similarity of sentiment may reinforce the conviction that only through the dark enveloping consciousness of nothingness is the highest hope available. But that same dark consciousness of insidious non-being, focused for us in the knowledge of death, if it cannot itself be made meaningful, will, as Camus so well understood, drain the meaning out of all particular projects, make to seem absurd even the limited values we can calculate on achieving in a short span of uncertain existence. The universal death penalty, as Camus called it, makes human life itself absurd, and his response, like Russell's, is defiance, the first reaction of *The Rebel*.

The second and more serious hazard, then, for the more modest of calculable goals is that they will not be able to silence the still, small, chilly voice of the enemy within, the persistent awareness of non-being, in order to be able to persuade their pursuers of their limited value. And it is a matter of praxis, and not a matter for theory, to decide whether such modest, calculable goals can or cannot manage to satisfy human beings and to regulate human behaviour without having to deal with death. I think it possible that they can, for at least some people, some of the time.

## Religion and war

What must be blindingly obvious, however, to anyone who considers the general conduct of human affairs, is that such modest aims are not the only regulators of human behaviour on this earth, nor are they even the most common. For people who threaten to kill or are prepared to die, whether by engagement in arms or by economic manoeuvres, not only deal with death directly and consciously, they also deal in death. The iron logic of the moral sense requires of them the candid admission that they are therefore dealing in moral absolutes and not in modest aims.

I cannot be asked to give my life, or ask another's, unless an absolute value is at stake, for I have nothing (quite literally) other than life to give; the absolute value, however it is described, must therefore entail a life that defeats death in all its manifest forms. Otherwise I am really being asked to commit myself to death itself, and that indeed, in the permanent presence of the fear *sui generis* which I face, is one of my deepest temptations: to collaborate with death in a sensual orgy of destruction, to gain some significance for my defeated life by the measure of my dedication to the destruction of life. Small men swaggering about with big guns know well what is meant here; so do some heavy drinkers, some of the incalculably rich, some people on the dole who ignore all healthy housekeeping advice because they can only give some spice to life by eating artificially flavoured junk food and smoking. There is nothing esoteric about this dark knowledge.

War is the most obtrusive, the most internationally advertised of the ways in which people, and indeed whole nations, deal in death. It can serve best, then, to illustrate the point that all who deal in death do, at least by implication, envisage moral absolutes, and the further point that moral absolutes require by their very nature a faith and a hope which rivals religious faith and hope in depth and comprehensiveness. For the invitation which so many nations presently issue to their populations to be prepared to kill or to die provides the clearest index to a people's true hierarchy of values, and also to the absoluteness of the commitment, the extent of the faith and hope that is expected in respect of the highest of their chosen values.

Take that last point first. The sense of obligation which accompanies every pursuit of value lays claim upon reality present and future, engages belief and hope in what can and will *be*. And the more of life that is committed to the pursuit of a value the larger that claim and the more comprehensive that belief and hope (and vice versa). If the life itself is to be sacrificed, then the claim, the faith, and the hope begin naturally to refer to a kind of life which is no longer threatened by death. This need not be construed as a crude kind of selfishness—I will only give up my life if I can be assured of a better one. I could conceivably give my life in order to gain, not a living continuity of my individual ego, but a better and less threatened future for whatever is good in me and in all other things. Practical commitment is in question here, not theoretical calculation, and I can only commit life to higher life, to life no longer corroded as it presently is by unresting death. Otherwise in giving my life I am merely dealing in death, and that is the anti-value, that is nihilism, the most deadly of all temptations and the one to which it is easiest to succumb. Now the faith and hope which forms the necessary spirit of such total commitment is religious in its depth and breadth, whether or not it avails itself of the traditional religious symbolism of eternal life, immortal beings, and impervious joy. I define as absolute a value for which I sacrifice life itself, for such a value is then not relative to any state or condition of human life which I could specify as worth sacrificing for it. It is absolute. If true morality is a matter of absolute values, then morality belongs with religion and Kolakowski is quite correct. If lesser moralities are possible, moralities which hide from death rather than meeting its pervasive challenge, Kolakowski's views might be modified. But the ubiquity of killing and of risking life in the attempt to kill, normally though not exclusively in war, nevertheless means that most moralities are of the absolute kind, and they positively invite us to enquire after the precise projects, aims or values which so many people apparently take to be absolute.

## The pursuit of absolute values

When I was young many men of my father's generation, I was told, had given their lives 'for Ireland', and my father could easily have lost his in the same cause. That seems clear enough on the face of it—until one tries to unpack that powerfully emotional phrase, 'for Ireland'. Considering the state of Ireland fifty years after the revolution, my father was often heard to wonder aloud why his comrades had given their lives. This was not, of course, to condone British Imperialism, which caused more cultural vandalism over the face of this earth than any relatively insignificant nation had ever before managed to inflict on so many. But it does serve to illustrate the way in which absolute status is so often claimed by political leaders for values which are then not easily defined.

The frequency with which successful liberation movements are followed by savage civil wars is history's own painful way of pressing home this same point. Today millions of people seem quite prepared to threaten all life on this planet for the sake of 'freedom' and 'democracy' on the one hand and a bright 'socialist' future for all humankind on the other; yet these highly emotional slogans are no more precise than is 'Ireland' or 'king and country'. Furthermore, a cold comparison of either of them with the inhuman exploitation of so many people who are driven through the very jaws of death on both sides of this great divide by very different forms of imperialism would quickly sap the enthusiasm for sacrifice which the propagandists on both sides seem so eager to maintain.

One of the factors involved in the sinister alchemy which changes imprecise emotions into absolute values is, undoubtedly, religious faith. Not one world religion, but apparently all, prove willing accomplices in war, as they do also in the lethal economic exploitation which can either act as a more effective substitute for war or actually lead to it.

Now it would of course be a cause of anger that a book on modern theology should meet the obvious need to consider a possible practical encounter of world religions by proposing to look first, and perhaps only, at their remote or immediate involvement with war. But it is as true of religions as it is of nation states or of great civilizations, that the shortest route to a true account of the values they consider absolute is found by asking them what are the causes they endorse for which one might kill or die. Introductory works must of their nature seek the shortest route, and in any case the issue of war has now become so crucial to the very survival of the human race that every religion must contribute to the ensuing debate its most distinctive vision. The current human crisis makes comparison inevitable at the same time as it dictates this context for comparison.

## *A survey of the world's main religions on the topic of war*

The clearest impression from the quickest survey of the main religions operative in the world is that they all of them in stated circumstances and in varying degrees endorse war while all, again in varying degrees, regret it and say all that can be said against it. Even the Baha'is find occasion for war, and that even after their united world authority has come into being. A statement addressed to the peoples of the world, issued from their Universal House of Justice in October 1985 and entitled *The Promise of World Peace*, contains this quotation concerning the great covenant of peace which is to be established: 'if any government later violate any one of its provisions, all the governments on earth should arise to reduce it to utter submission, nay the human race as a whole should resolve, with every power at its disposal, to destroy that government.'[5] Now that is fighting talk, and the provision laid down earlier in the same pamphlet, in a quotation from Shoghi Effendi to the effect that every nation must cede *in favour of the super-state* every claim to make war and all rights to maintain armaments, 'except for purposes of maintaining internal order', simply implies that war is now the prerogative of the whole against recalcitrant parts. It is war in pursuit of peace, of course, but then what war was ever described otherwise?

The Islamic doctrine of jihad is probably familiar to most people today, if only through those extremist interpretations which motivate the more militant Muslim revivalists. Sura II, 190 of the Holy Qur'an, which contains a divine command to fight, is variously translated: 'Fight in the cause of God those who fight you, but do not transgress limits', and 'Fight in the way of Allah against those who fight against you, but begin not hostilities' (translations by Abdullah Yusuf Ali and Mohammed Marmaduke Pickthall respectively). But such differences in translation merely mirror a more general disagreement concerning the conditions under which a Muslim may, with the sanction of his faith, take up arms; they do nothing to diminish the force of the positive implication that warfare may be used for the defence of the faith itself.

One of the titles of the God that Jews worship (and Christians also) is Yahweh of Hosts or Lord of Armies. The words which Deuteronomy 7: 16 places on his lips sound much more indiscriminate than the verse of the Qur'an and depict him as a right savage old warlord: 'You shall destroy all the peoples that the Lord your God will give into your hands; your eye shall not pity them.' There are, of course, within both Judaism and Christianity theological strategies for reducing the authority of such savagely indiscriminate edicts and for regulating the option and conduct of warfare, but unless central features of the life and death of Jesus are emphasized which, in my view, would question all such busy military moralizing, there is none that altogether renounces the use of arms.

The great Hindu religion is so old and so richly developed that it is not difficult to find within its more theistic forms the face of a god of war. Interesting mutations of the attitude to war and peace do, however, sometimes accompany some of the religious movements which grew from the Hindu matrix at the precipitation of heterodox ascetics such as Gautama, Mahavira, and, much later, Guru Nanak. Buddhism of its nature seeks a transcendence of the self, and hence of all selfishness and strife, but since it is a kind of liberation that seeks to escape the relative 'unreality' of the empirical rather than to transform it, it is difficult to get from a Buddhist *roshi* a clear ruling about warfare, other than the general regrets about its occasional inevitability which most religions express, together with the solemn warning that wilful engagement in warfare destroys, or at least delays, all progress in 'the way'.

The Jains, followers of Mahavira, certainly took the Hindu virtue of *ahimsa* to extremes unequalled by any other religious tradition. The Hindu spokesman to whom I referred explained that *ahimsa* really meant the absence of anger or animosity, and that warfare could be used for socially therapeutic purposes, to cut out some evil from the human community, provided no personal hatred was involved. But Jains seem determined to avoid harm to any form of life; even inadvertent harm must be confessed as guilt, and life for them is in everything that

exists. I am not sure if Jains have ever taken up arms in self-
defence, or how they explained this if they did, and the fact that
they are so prominently represented amongst the mercantile
classes makes me wonder how they can manage to stay pure in a
world in which the military-industrial complex creeps into all the
nooks and crannies of the world economy, and in which economic forces themselves are amongst the most sophisticated
weapons of violent oppression. However all that may be, the
Jains certainly come closest to the total renunciation of armed
violence of any organized religion, and it is no accident that
Gandhi's religious philosophy of non-violence was directly influenced by the saintly Jain sadhus whom he met in his youth.

The Sikh religion has followed a very different course. It was
founded by the Hindu Guru Nanak at the beginning of the sixteenth century AD, in near despair at the atrocities of Muslim
raids and Hindu reactions and at the superficiality and divisive-
ness of so much that passed for religion; its founder sought to
bring about such human reconciliation (at first *without* founding
an 'extra' religion) that there would be 'no longer Hindu or
Musulman'. But within a century its sixth Guru, at his investi-
ture, was to strap on two swords to represent his spiritual and
temporal power (Pope Boniface VIII did the same in 1302, but
only symbolically, in writing), and he later organized a standing
army. From the time of the tenth Guru, Gobind Singh, a two-
edged sword was used in the Sikh initiation ceremony, and Sikhs
to this day engage in armed conflict in pursuit of their religio-
political aims.

And Christians, with whom this book is primarily concerned?
In taking the authoritative Jewish Scriptures with them across the
chasm that unfortunately developed, the followers of Jesus the
Jew inherited also the warlord image of God which is so prominent in these Scriptures. And yet, in spite of that, there is more
than ample evidence to suggest that for at least two centuries a
majority of the early followers of Jesus understood their discipleship to imply a farewell to arms. They knew that enlisting in
armies involved a religious or quasi-religious commitment.
Instead of dismissing their stance today on the grounds of the
obsolescence of such an understanding of warfare, we shall have

to rediscover the truth of it. But the point, in any case, is the more positive one that to them following Jesus prohibited any infliction of injury or death upon others, and rendered professions likely to be involved in such activities inaccessible to them.

Christians, of course, succeeded to a level of political leadership in the Roman Empire which the Emperor Constantine, who issued the Edict of Toleration in AD 314, could scarcely have envisaged—if he had envisaged it, he might have thought again about toleration! However, it must be allowed that it was Christians who saved all that was best in that ancient and most formative civilization of the Western world. Long before Boniface used the symbolism of the two swords to assert his authority over the civil rulers, something called Christendom had come about in Europe: such an embodiment of Christian faith in all of secular culture that no separation could be envisaged much before the rise of modern democracies in France and the United States of America. And still, long after the coming of the Age of Reason and the rise of these democracies, a variety of forms survived and developed for the closest relationship of Christian communities and secular governments. At one extreme is the Vatican, still a tiny sovereign state sending its ambassadors around the world; at the other the Moral Majority and its successor in the United States of America, a well-organized group of Christians from different churches, exercising what it chooses to describe as moral influence upon that country's legislature. And through all these centuries and changing civic structures Christianity has endorsed war—*just* war, of course—blessed armies, celebrated victories with loud *Te Deums*, and displayed in its sanctuaries the flags of battles old and new.

Since the age of European expansion in the sixteenth and seventeenth centuries the very spread of Christianity often accompanied the military and mercantile colonialists, and though Christian missionaries often sought to counter the excesses of these rapacious men, they seldom if ever spoke against the use of arms as such. Today quite a few Christian spokespersons insist that all nuclear warfare is immoral by nature, that there could be no such thing as a just nuclear war. This conclusion, however, even if its logic could be secured, is for Christians too convenient by half, since the onus of proof lies upon the indiscriminate and incalculable destructiveness of nuclear weapons, and not upon the power of the Christian faith itself to provide alternative means of solving human problems. It is therefore in a very real sense convenient for Christians that nuclear weapons threaten such horrors: it exonerates them from clearing up their attitudes to war as such; it exonerates them in particular from the need to confess that of all the values which the first Christians held dear and which their successors in moods of reformation admitted to having betrayed, the renunciation of violence has not been listed.

The point of that brief whirlwind tour of world religions is not to engage in any invidious comparisons between them, but rather to illustrate the extent of endorsement of war by religions— hedged about as such endorsement always is by the most careful statement of conditions. For it is the simple fact of such general religious endorsement of warfare that raises the questions that now finally concern us.

First, what role does religious faith or its substitutes play in the ability of modern states to wage war or to prepare whole populations to do so? Second, what implications does such endorsement have for religious faith itself, and for the God who is its source and object? And, lastly, can any religion, even at this late stage of development of an increasingly suicidal race, offer any viable alternative?

## The role of religious faith in justifying war

First, then, the argument still stands that since I have nothing greater than life itself to commit to any cause, the cause which may require my very life of me must contain the hope of a life which death no longer threatens. Otherwise such total commitment would have to be judged irrational, and more sinister motivation for my self-destruction would have to be sought. Now there can be little or no doubt that religions have always supplied to soldiers of almost every nation just this kind of hope, and that by doing so they have helped make the commitment of life itself to the wars of nations seem justified. This is an extremely useful part of the service which religions offer to the civil states with which they enter into such varied kinds of relationships, and it goes a long way to explain the chagrin of governments when religious leaders prove less than totally enthusiastic about some of their war efforts. A just war morality which has the consent of a church can, for any soldier who has in any way been convinced of the justice of his violent engagement, add to his expectation of a gain of territory, or of more acceptable structures of government, or of other comparable amenities, the hope of eternal life. In the absence of this enormous hope, on the other hand, leaders who wish to persuade people to kill and to die would have to elevate to a level of absoluteness at which they could rival religious values whatever aims they have in view, or can pretend to have in view, in waging war.

It is at this point that it becomes questionable whether such alternative absolutes can bear much analysis of their concrete and measurable contents. It is therefore left to the powerful tool of propaganda to marshall human emotions to cover over the holes left by a departed religion in the vision of an acceptable human destiny. It is significant that such propaganda so often uses the images and symbols of a rejected religion: Hitler did this with astounding success when he surrounded himself with the copied paraphernalia of the Holy Roman Empire, and many a communist vision of the future carries intriguing reminiscences of the communion of saints at the end of history.

Human motivation is usually mixed, of course, and probably never so mixed as it must surely be in any human being who contemplates the most extreme of all actions, to kill another human being and to be prepared to die in the attempt to do so. Part of that motivation may be the temptation which fear breeds, the temptation to servile status: in the case of the pervasive fear of death the temptation to become death's willing servant, to take pleasure in dealing death. That is the motivation that seems to have directed Hitler's last days, and to have infected those closest to him, and nobody who contemplates killing can be altogether immune from it. Mixed or not, however, the motivation to kill and to be prepared to die in the attempt inevitably involves either the siren voices of nihilism or the pursuit of values so absolute that they make religious or quasi-religious claims upon reality.

Thus the role of religions and of their genuine secular substitutes in appearing to secure these claims by holding out hopes of the required absolutes, the happy eternities, has always provided essential support to every military campaign.

## The implications for religion, and our view of God

What the second question asks, then, is what implications does providing such support have for religious faith. The answer must be that since it enables a group, national or otherwise, to act in God's name, it binds God's honour to the aims of that group and to the methods used to achieve those aims. If morality in the act of killing inevitably reaches the religious dimension, then religion in the course of conflict absorbs into its own content the goals and methods of the combatants. If the goals invoked enjoin killing others, or dying in the attempt to kill others, in pursuit of, say, sovereignty over some land in the South Atlantic or access to oil in the Middle East, then such things as sovereignty and access to oil and killing for them and dying in the course of killing for them are nothing less than ways to God, for God has decreed such ways, however reluctantly God may be conceived to have done so, and those who follow God's decree must come to God.

To what God shall they come? To a warlord. To a warlord, moreover, who is as biased as all warlords must be, who fights for one group of human beings. The only difference between an old Viking wanting to die in the heat of battle in order to go straight to Valhalla and a modern infantryman is the latter's half-faith, the product of an age of superficial doubt, which flares into an equally idolatrous flame only when the spark of the final fear of death ignites it; the only difference between the priest of Odin and a modern priest blessing a modern army is that the former was clear and honest about his god while the latter does his familiar soft-shoe shuffle between his war-god and his pathetic little bleat about justice, and peace, and sometimes even love.

The shuffle is designed to disguise the fact that no earthly form of justice can require human life, and no heavenly form of justice can be expected from a god who dispenses human life for earthly forms of justice. To expect such would be similar to, though infinitely more foolish than, expecting men of violence to bring peace and justice to a society from which they will by violence wrest the power of its present rulers. Those who kill with the sword to achieve changes in society will live by the sword when they do achieve them. The means of achieving their aims against present opposition will be the means of securing them against any future opposition. And those who live by the sword will in their turn die by the sword. Like Barabbas and Pilate, and Caiaphas. And peace and justice can never come. There is every reason to suspect that a god who enjoins the taking of life for temporal ends, which cannot of their nature justify such sacrifice, would be as incapable of securing peace and justice either here or hereafter as any of his terrestrial lieutenants.

It is important to recognize that the force of the point does not in the least depend upon the obviously immoral atrocities comitted by all sides in every known war. It depends, rather, on the point that the taking of life cannot be justified, and the losing of life can only be borne, in the part-experience, part-hope of a life over which death no longer has any dominion. Once that point is taken, it becomes obvious that the distinction between primitive religions and world religions is in its usual implications highly questionable. Most if not all religions and quasi-religions are primitive, in that they endorse war and preparation for war, and thus present to this beleaguered race a veritable rogue's gallery of divine warlords.

It may seem, as I move now towards the third question, as to whether religions can offer a viable alternative to the suicidal manner in which the human race now settles its differences, that some phrases have already slipped in to nudge attention in the general direction of Christianity. It is necessary, therefore, to be quite clear that I do look to Christianity in quest of such an alternative for the very simple reason that Christianity is all I really know. I do also believe that my Christian faith has betrayed both God and humanity in the matter now under discussion, and that it has done this as successfully as any other form of human faith has ever done it. Any alternatives that are found in the Christian source-vision I see as a challenge to other religions to find something comparable, rather than an indictment of any of them. What must not be lost from sight is the simple fact that life-and-death issues lead directly to beliefs and hopes that have a religious depth to them, and that there is therefore no more direct route, and no more necessary route to follow in today's world, to the heart of any religion and to that part of it that all religions must now quite honestly bare to each other and to the whole of humanity.

## The Christian alternative

The root causes of war, the basic motivations that persuade people to go to war, or even to prepare for it, are sometimes difficult to detect amongst the welter of emotions and half-reasons, pressures and illusions, which usually conspire to bring into being this essentially self-defeating enterprise. The romance of death itself, the illusory heroism of the obscene act of killing so artfully sustained through martial pomp and circumstance, the lying propaganda inevitably spread by each side about the other: all of these are surely always amongst the contributory factors, but none provides the root cause or the basic motive. This must come from deeper reaches of the relationships which bind people to each other and to the common earth which most immediately sustains them all.

There can be little doubt that the root cause of war lies in relations of production which are as yet unredeemed because deeper within these very fundamental relations lie relations of absolute dependence upon material things which turn both sides of the relationship into flesh (or infuse both with a destructive, demonic spirit). Such dependence, with its consequent clinging and grasping, by which mortals attempt to sustain themselves upon things as transitory as themselves, reduplicates dread, a fear like no other fear, and it is out of fear that people kill.

There is a peculiar paradox of ownership according to which the more totally and exclusively one tries to own part of our common world, the more one treats ownership of it as an unconditional (absolute) right or value, the more one tries to control it, the more it owns and controls its owner. This is but a particular version of the master–slave relationship and of its topsy-turvy logic which many a philosophical commentator has noticed.

There is a particularly frightening poetic version of it in one of Borges' stories, about a dagger which once used as a murder weapon begins to take on a life of its own and to seek out occasions and people to use it to kill again and again.

Property can use people too; it can even use them to kill each other in its name. People fight for their country. Land is thus deified, and becomes the warlord. Once again the so-called primitive religions were more honest about this than their modern counterparts, ecclesiastic or civil, when they actually deified lands. The ancient mother goddess of the Irish Celts was actually the island personified, and little Filipino schoolchildren were heard on television recently singing to the world that no invaders would tread on their sacred shores. People who look down their noses at primitive religions are staring at clay models of themselves. The land, of course, will suffer destruction too, as much as both sides can inflict on it, in the course of the conflict it causes, because it is as true of things as it is of people that the wielder of the sword will perish by the sword.

The same topsy-turvy logic re-emerges at the level of relationships between person and person if only because, as Marx noted, unredeemed relations of production make commodities of all those who engage in them. Those who control the means of production thus control the people-commodities, the labouring masses. The latter are as the rest of the property owned, similarly absolutized to the point where they will be fought over, and a similar logic prevails whereby they become in the end the ones who actually conduct the battle and are destroyed in it. Amongst the heroes of my school-days were the old warlords from the North of Ireland, the O'Neills and the O'Donnells, who swept down through the country to final defeat at the Battle of Kinsale. Only later did I learn through more critical history that they used the common people with contempt—*criadhairi* they called them, a word for peasants constructed from the word for clay—for *their* burnt-earth policy involved destroying peasants and crops alike! In every war it is the have-nots, the ones who are owned who, in addition to the humiliation of being turned from the commodities they already are into robotic appendages to weapons of war, suffer the brunt of the carnage of the war itself. When a large jet carrying American soldiers home on furlough crashed in Newfoundland recently, killing all on board, the newscaster commented in his most professional matter-of-fact tone that most of those who died were poor blacks from the southern states of America, since the majority of front-line troops in the American army were drawn from the poorer classes.

When in the course of war or of threats of violence people's values inevitably become absolutized, it is only those who are still duped by the persistent propaganda who can fail to see the true hierarchy of a people's values, and the injustice writ large. Religions are inevitably involved wherever absolutes wield their awful influence; and whether they be primitive religions, or world religions, or their modern substitutes, they are equally guilty of the ensuing injustice and of the betrayal of the true absolute whose conventional name is God.

The point of the preceding paragraphs is not to analyse the anatomy of war, or even to illustrate once again the contention that it is relationships to things and to people which lie even deeper within Marx's relations of production which render the latter unredeemed and possibly irredeemable. The point, rather, is to prove that the alternative to violence, if such there be, must be sought first in the more general relationships which are formed in the commonest of human activities and not in those relationships and activities which are especially formed in the war arena itself, or in immediate preparations to meet armed violence. Once the arming of people begins, once weapons are manufactured and stockpiled in readiness, once the inevitable accompanying propaganda is in place, the alternative has obviously already been missed. Those who talk of alternatives to war are commonly asked what they would have done when Hitler threatened to invade their country. The question, one must admit, is usually a trump card; but only because if forces one to think in terms of meeting force by force, by focusing attention on imminent preparation for war, and keeping attention once more away from the more common ways of living in which the alternative can be found. For only if fear is eradicated from the family meal, will it fail to control one's actions when the armed soldier arrives in fear to break down one's door.

*Eucharistic praxis: the Christian training to die*

The power that could overcome the spirit of violence, whose body is death-spewing armour and its human appendages, must be a mighty power indeed, but it could not succeed if it did not transform first our most elementary relationships to our world and our daily relationships with our fellow humans. And that brings us back to bread which, as the Eucharistic prayer puts it, 'earth has given and human hands have made'. In *Eucharistic* taking of bread, symbol and earnest of all that the world gives, is the power of all-pervasive grace which to Christians is the presence of God, that is to say, the spirit of Jesus. In the breaking of bread to others, symbol and earnest of that permanent openness to them which gift and grace inspires, is the training to die of which Plato spoke. This training to die is the antidote to war. People are persuaded to die in war, certainly, but only in the attempt to kill others. Killing is the primary intent in war; people die for their countries only in the attempt to kill for their countries. War is always the expression of the power of death. But to train in Eucharist to die for others rather than to kill is the expression of the power of life. For in Eucharist the power of gift enables one to die in the most ordinary action of daily life, the meal, in order that that which comes as grace should pass through one's selfless self to others. In Eucharist, provided that the special meal is simply the paradigm for all meals and for all other dealings with others, and provided that the table is closed to no one, dying is in the service of life, whereas in war life is put at the service of death. Eucharistic praxis, therefore, is the Christian alternative to war. It is also, this book has argued, the essence of Christianity, which Christians have most commonly betrayed.

The failure of this power in the world, the age-old complicity of Christians in war, is due to a lack of faith, a failure of that particular form of human religious faith which is the conviction of ultimate grace (in Mark 8: 11–12, this lack of faith is presented as a lack of understanding of Eucharist). But the failure has not been universal, and at times Christians have actually demonstrated the superiority of grace over arms. We have seen on our television screens in recent times masses of unarmed people standing between President Marcos' heavily armed troops and their intended, heavily armed victims, offering to both flowers and food, and securing in this way a (temporary) conversion of the violent. The scenes were reminiscent of others, of Czechoslovakia in 1968 where a conversion was not recorded and is not recorded . . . yet, and of Gandhi, who proved that the power of this kind of faith, which Christians believe could bring about peace and justice, can find echoes in other religious traditions. In these and similar incidents a praxis emerges in history which could do more for *rapprochement* between the religions and substitute religions of the world than either theological agreements or institutional embassies could ever achieve. But this eucharistic praxis needs to become more common, and to transform a whole web of human relationships which presently link the family table to the battle-ground—I mean the web of economic relationships in modern society where belligerent competition is the only recognized spirit, where some succeed only at the expense of others, where the standard of living for some sounds the death-knell for many and the quality of life is thereby diminished for all, where the large gesture of generosity from the rich countries still operates, however necessary it may be to stave off starvation for some and pangs of conscience for others, as a substitute for justice for all.

A power and a presence that can deal with everything from the jaws of death to such ebb-tides of life as boredom and surfeit? Christians believe, or they ought to believe, that it can be encountered in their eucharistic fellowship, at least on the few occasions on which Eucharist is truly celebrated as a sacrament of all existence. For they believe that there is encountered a spirit, a presence, which history in its larger mood can quite easily identify as that which was embodied in the life and death of Jesus of Nazareth; a power and a presence to which some of Jesus' followers then and now give the divine name, in the conviction and the hope that it is the self-emptying power of creation, the inner secret of all reality, the grace that rules the universe, 'the love that moves the sun and the other stars'.

\* \* \*

'Yes, yes, but what about *me*?' cries a little voice from deep inside the author (and perhaps the reader also), 'surely you cannot end this book with these fine-sounding echoes of Bloch and Dante and not say a little more clearly what is to become of *me*?'

You, a possible reply might run, are an ego that has still not quite become a self. You have not yet faced up to what you are, a self that can be and live as a self only in the course of the necessary process of recognizing the other as truly other, and not as an extension of self which turns you back into an ego again. But once you become a self in the course of this necessary process, you recognize the difference, the gap between you and others, the spaceless, timeless chasm into which one or both of you may fall. You become reflectively self-conscious, and the dark shapeless mass of nothingness enters into your awareness of everything; in fact it allows you to see 'everything', 'world', 'universe' in all its common promise and common fragility. And at that moment the most basic choice of all awaits you: to grasp at finite things to sustain yourself, to turn them into extensions of self and so become all ego again; or to pour out to the other all that comes from self, and from other to enrich self, and in the very pouring out to experience an enrichment of self that ego could never have thought possible.

You must not imagine, however, that such a choice can be made by sheer dint of mental calculation. It needs a unique and enormous power to enable you to choose that second option: the first is far more natural, in an original sense of the word natural in which it refers to that with which you were born. If you are lucky enough to encounter that self-giving power called grace, either in other people or at the heart of all ordinary things, then the choice of that second option becomes a possibility. You may believe that you have encountered the immanence of God, and then the following sketchy account may be offered of what will become of you.

You will live without that deep, pervasive fear which feeds the ordinary fears of all specific things, and without which the ordinary fears of strangers and of pain, of the night and of empty places, will cease to rule you. Then, free from the rule of fear, you will not arouse the fears and thence the hostility of others. You might even manage to live in this world without fear, and the joy of that simple fact would be immeasurable.

You will appreciate, quite literally, quite insignificant things. An old pair of shoes will breathe out the beauty of the service they have given, will solicit some care still, and when they are finally past serving will pass on something of the spirit of service as they are consigned with some parting sorrow to the rubbish dump. The very rubbish dump will be transformed, for everything that ever served should be given a decent burial.

Loaves will multiply when given rather than grabbed. There will seem to be—for indeed there always is—more than enough of everything for everybody.

You will begin to recognize the spirit of grace in certain economic and political programmes, and its absence or even its opposite in others. Schemes designed to give workers a share in the ownership of their industry and make their products more their own creation for others; political initiatives such as Willi Brandt's for reducing the growing chasm between rich and poor countries by rearranging political priorities—such programmes will commend themselves. You will become more political, not by uncritical allegiance to any party or programme where you again become a yes-person, a voice in the sense of a vote that can be counted (on), another appendage to another machine; but by recognizing that the kingdom of grace was always meant for this world and that all programmes must always be reshaped by its spirit.

You will realize how very few people and programmes, how very few days and actions of your own life, embody this spirit. You will come to see the Christian community in the world as the greatest unmobilized force for good that the world has ever known. You will see the narrowness of the Eucharistic tables as you have never seen it before, and in the same vision in which you see that you can break the Eucharistic bread with other religions as validly as Jewish followers of Jesus once took the equally enormous step of breaking it with Gentiles, you will see the entombing of the spirit of Jesus in the very act which should free it from the grave of history.

You will become acutely aware of the endemic violence of all modern societies, an economic form of violence visited daily upon myriads of the poor and the starving. It is a violence more effective than arms, as the new empires of the 'free' world quite obviously understand; its effectiveness often culminates in armed conflict, and armed conflict then provides a clear mirror-image of the privileges and the injustices it seeks to perpetuate (the poor are persuaded to kill the poor). And you will notice your own daily complicity in this endemic violence of modern society, and in these more general terms the failure of the lives of Christians to be truly Eucharistic, breaking the bread of life to others, and so learning to die in order that all might have life and life more abundant. And you will see in this daily failure the cause of the more specific failure to find any power alternative to violence with which to meet the violent person when he or she comes to kill.

You will know that a true follower of Jesus can only die in order to live, but can never kill, or prepare to kill, or even prepare to die in the effort to kill. And you will remember how many Christian soldiers have marched onward to their sad and mistaken deaths for over sixteen centuries, sometimes with the cross of Jesus emblazoned on their chests in the final betrayal of his cause.

But you will not despair, for grace is the fertile mother of hope. You will not fear your own death, for in every selfless act of self-enrichment you will have drawn its sting. You will not be able to see beyond the gentle earth into which, like your old shoes, you too must go; but the cold will be cool refreshment now, and the darkness restful, the grassy folds of the earth inviting. You cannot know now, you who ask so anxiously whether what lies beyond that final anabasis will be bodily or spiritual, or if such distinctions make more real sense 'hereafter' than they make here. But such information is not necessary for you now. It is hidden in the depths of God in which you are learning to live.

You will be all right.

# Suggested Reading and Notes

## Chapter 1

*Suggested reading*

A. J. Ayer, *Language, Truth and Logic* (London, 1946)

R. Bultmann, 'The Primitive Christian Kerygma and the Historical Jesus' in eds. C. E. Braaten and R. A. Harrisville, *The Historical Jesus and the Kerygmatic Christ* (Nashville, 1964)

H. Butterfield, *Christianity and History* (London, 1949)

F. Gerald Downing, *Has Christianity a Revelation?* (London, 1964)

A. Flew, *God and Philosophy* (London, 1966)

Van A. Harvey, *The Historian and the Believer* (London, 1967)

James P. Mackey, ed., *Religious Imagination* (Edinburgh, 1986)

James M. Robinson, *A New Quest of the Historical Jesus* (London, 1959)

A. Schweitzer, *The Quest of the Historical Jesus* (London, 1954)

Mary Warnock, *Imagination* (London, 1976)

Of a quite different order of difficulty from the above are:

H. Gadamer, *Truth and Method* (London, 1975)

M. Heidegger, *Being and Time* (London, 1962)

M. Merleau-Ponty, *The Phenomenology of Perception* (London, 1962)

*Notes*

1. M. Heidegger, *An Introduction to Metaphysics* (New York, 1961), p. 6.

2. Wallace Stevens, *Collected Poems* (London and New York). This extract is reprinted here by permission of Faber and Faber Ltd and Alfred A. Knopf Inc.

3. Oscar Wilde, *De Profundis* (London, 1911), p. 71.

4. James Scully, *Modern Poets on Modern Poetry* (London, 1966),

p. 22. The verses of poetry are from Yeats's 'The Rose upon the Rood of Time'.

5.  J. P. Sartre, *Existentialism and Humanism* (London, 1966), p. 56.

## Chapter 2

### Suggested reading

E. Bloch, *Man on His Own* (New York, 1971)

John R. Donahue, *Are you the Christ?* (Missoula, 1973)

L. Feuerbach, *The Essence of Christianity* (New York, 1957)

W. Kelber, *The Passion in Mark* (Philadelphia, 1976)

D. McLellan, *Karl Marx: Selected Writings* (Oxford, 1977)

K. Marx, F. Engels, *On Religion* (Moscow, 1955)

### Notes

1.  G. W. F. Hegel, *Early Theological Writings* (Chicago, 1948), p. 38.

2.  Mary Warnock, *Imagination* (London, 1976), p. 10.

3.  L. Feuerbach, *The Essence of Christianity* (New York, 1957), p. 21.

4.  Ibid., p. 32.

5.  K. Marx, F. Engels, *On Religion* (Moscow, 1955), p. 41.

6.  Ibid., p. 241.

7.  D. McLellan, *Karl Marx: Selected Writings* (Oxford, 1977), pp. 156 ff.

8.  Ibid., p. 79.

9.  Ibid., p. 80.

10. Ibid., p. 82.

11. Ibid., pp. 121–2.

12. See text and commentary in N. Lash, *A Matter of Hope: A Theologian's Reflections on the Thought of Karl Marx* (London, 1981), pp. 115 ff.

13. Marx, Engels, *On Religion*, p. 42.

14. Philip Larkin's 'Aubade' first appeared in the December 1977 issue of the *Times Literary Supplement*. They are reprinted here by permission of Faber and Faber Ltd.

15. E. Bloch, *Man on His Own* (New York, 1971), p. 48.

16. Ibid., p. 41.

17. John R. Donahue, *Are you the Christ*? (Missoula, 1973), pp. 222 ff.

## Chapter 3

*Suggested reading*

L. Bouyer, *Eucharist* (U. of Notre Dame, 1968)

R. H. Fuller, *The Formation of the Resurrection Narratives* (London, 1971)

Walter Kasper, *Jesus the Christ* (London, 1976)

Hans Küng, *On Being a Christian* (London, 1976)

John McKenna, *Eucharist and Holy Spirit* (Great Wakering, 1975)

E. Schillebeeckx, *Jesus: An Experiment in Christology* (London, 1979)

*Notes*

1. L. Bouyer, *Eucharist* (Univ. of Notre Dame, 1968), p. 149.
2. Theodore of Mopsuestia, *Mystagogical Catechesis*, vi. 11–13.

## Chapter 4

*Suggested reading*

R. Brown, *The Birth of the Messiah* (London, 1977)

Josephus, *Jewish Antiquities* in *The Complete Works of Fhavius Josephus* (Chicago, 1913)

James P. Mackey, *Jesus, the Man and the Myth* (London, 1979)

N. Perrin, *Rediscovering the Teaching of Jesus* (New York, 1967)

## Chapter 5

*Suggested reading*

Walter M. Abbott, ed., *The Documents of Vatican II* (London, 1966)

*Anglican–Roman Catholic International Commission: The Final Report* (London, 1982)

*Baptism, Eucharist and Ministry* (Faith and Order Paper no. 11, Geneva, 1982)

Karl Barth, *Church Dogmatics*, Vol. I, part 1, and Vol II, part 2 (Edinburgh, 1975)

J. D. G. Dunn, *Jesus and the Spirit* (London, 1975)

H. Fries, K. Rahner, *Unity of the Churches: a Real Possibility* (New York, 1985)

H. Küng, *The Structures of the Church* (London, 1965)

James P. Mackey, *The Christian Experience of God as Trinity* (London, 1983)

E. Schillebeeckx, *The Church with a Human Face* (London, 1985)

*Notes*

1. J. D. G. Dunn, *Jesus and the Spirit* (London, 1975), pp. 322, 323, 325.
2. *Documents of Vatican II*, Constitution on The Church, n. 18.
3. The Roman Catholic *Ecumenical Directory* (Catholic Truth Society, London, 1967).
4. ARCIC, *The Final Report*, p. 120.

## Chapter 6

*Suggested reading*

R. H. Bainton, *Christian Attitudes Towards War and Peace* (London, 1961)

A. Camus, *The Rebel* (London, 1962)

John Ferguson, *War and Peace in the World's Religions* (London, 1977)

L. Kolakowski, *Religion* (Fontana paperback, 1982)

P. Rieff, *The Triumph of the Therapeutic* (New York, 1968)

B. F. Skinner, *Beyond Freedom and Dignity* (New York, 1971)

*Notes*

1. K. Barth, *Dogmatics in Outline* (London, 1949), p. 46.
2. K. Marx, *The Poverty of Philosophy* (Peking, 1978), p. 115.
3. L. Kolakowski, *Religion* (Fontana paperback, 1982), p. 211.
4. *The Poems of Gerard Manley Hopkins* (Oxford, 4th edn., 1967; 1970).
5. From the Baha'i pamphlet, *The Promise of World Peace* (Haifa, 1985), pp. 20-1.

# Index

**OXFORD**

## MORE OXFORD PAPERBACKS

Details of a selection of other books follow. A complete list of Oxford Paperbacks, including The World's Classics, Twentieth-Century Classics, OPUS, Past Masters, Oxford Authors, Oxford Shakespeare, and Oxford Paperback Reference, is available in the UK from the General Publicity Department, Oxford University Press (JH), Walton Street, Oxford OX2 6DP.

In the USA, complete lists are available from the Paperbacks Marketing Manager, Oxford University Press, 200 Madison Avenue, New York, NY 10016.

Oxford Paperbacks are available from all good bookshops. In case of difficulty, customers in the UK can order direct from Oxford University Press Bookshop, 116 High Street, Oxford, Freepost, OX1 4BR, enclosing full payment. Please add 10 per cent of published price for postage and packing.

## IN THE VATICAN

### Peter Hebblethwaite

What really happens in the Vatican is often as surprising as it is fascinating. Peter Hebblethwaite reveals the secrets of its inner workings, as well as giving an insight into top-level Vatican thinking on such issues as priests and politics, and ecumenism. Most of all the book reveals what the recent popes were really like as men and, in particular, gives a fascinating portrait of the enigmatic present pope, John Paul II.

'brilliant . . . a fascinating evaluation of the present papacy' Peter Nicholls in the *Times*

'the most urbane, sad, funny and erudite commentary now available on the Vatican' *Guardian*

## JUDAISM

### Nicholas de Lange

'It is no mean feat to encompass all of Judaism in 150 pages. It is quite extraordinary to do it well, but Nicholas de Lange has achieved just that . . . he points gently towards dialogue and understanding, and has made a significant contribution towards it with this book.'
Julia Neuberger in the *Times Educational Supplement*